BETWEEN MIND AND BRAIN

BETWEEN MIND AND BRAIN
Models of the Mind and Models in the Mind

Ronald Britton

Routledge
Taylor & Francis Group

LONDON AND NEW YORK

First edition published 2015 by Karnac Books Ltd.

Published 2018 by Routledge
2 Park Square, Milton Park, Abingdon, Oxon OX14 4RN
711 Third Avenue, New York, NY 10017, USA

Routledge is an imprint of the Taylor & Francis Group, an informa business

British Library Cataloguing in Publication Data

A C.I.P. for this book is available from the British Library

ISBN-13: 9781782202608 (pbk)

Typeset by V Publishing Solutions Pvt Ltd., Chennai, India

To Jean,
for her encouragement and our shared love of psychoanalysis

CONTENTS

ACKNOWLEDGEMENTS

I have learnt so much from the clinical discussions I have had with psychoanalytic colleagues in so many different countries in the last thirty years. In this country I have benefitted from sharing ideas and case discussions with my colleagues in the British Psychoanalytical Society and the British Psychoanalytical Association. In particular, with my friends John Steiner and Michael Feldman with whom I have shared the annual West Lodge Conferences for the last twenty years and with fellow members of what was the Betty Joseph workshop and is now the Hillfield Road workshop.

Several chapters first saw the light of day in earlier versions as lectures: Chapter One at the Science Museum London, Chapter Five as a public lecture at the Institute of Psychoanalysis, London, Chapter Eight originally was a response to an invitation from the Psychoanaltyic Quarterly to participate in a discussion on the "Third in Psychoanalysis" in 2004, Chapter Eleven was a lecture to the Midland branch of the Jungian Society (SAP), to the Swiss Psychoanalytic Society Geneva, and at the "Festival of Ideas 2013" in Valparaiso, Chile; and Chapter Twelve was a public lecture at the Tavistock Clinic, London. I am grateful to all those institutions for inviting me.

ABOUT THE AUTHOR

Ronald Britton is a well-known international psychoanalytic writer who has lectured widely in Europe, North and South America. He was President of the British Psycho-Analytical Society and a Vice-President of the International Psychoanalytical Association. He has a predominantly clinical approach but also a special interest in the relationship of psychoanalysis to literature, philosophy and theology. He received the IPA Outstanding Scientific Achievement Award 2013, and the Sigourney Award for Outstanding Contributions to Psychoanalysis 2014.

INTRODUCTION

"In every writer on philosophy there is a concealed metaphysic, usually unconscious; even if his subject is metaphysics, he is almost certain to have an uncritically believed system which underlies his specific arguments."

—*Bertrand Russell* (Ayer & O'Grady, 1992, p. 389)

The quotation above applies equally to metapsychology, meta-neurology, and meta-linguistics. It is not, however, a reason for giving up metapsychology, nor can we give up our unconscious metapsychology; the psychoanalytic approach is to get to know the unconscious not to try fruitlessly to abolish it. Unconscious beliefs are treated as facts; they can only be evaluated once it is realised that they are not facts but assumptions. "Reality testing" may support them or contradict them. If experience and or reason produce an idea that coincides with an already existing unconscious belief this will be ego syntonic and then be held with a supreme degree of conviction. If experience contradicts an unconscious belief it will by no means be eradicated until it is repeatedly exposed as fallacious; even then it is likely to linger in the shadows waiting for a chance beam of external daylight to fall on it. As Freud described (1919h) we then have an "uncanny" (*unheimlich*) experience, sometimes déjà vu, sometimes experienced as if we have seen a ghost. This applies when an old belief has been overcome but not relinquished in the unconscious.

The implication of that tenacity is that a proportion of the reason for the retention of any belief is from the pleasure principle and not the reality principle. When the proportion is high the belief is an illusion whether it corresponds with external reality or not, according to Freud in *The Future of an Illusion* (1927c).

In this book I make out the case for abandoning Freud's economic version of the "pleasure principle" (1920g) which he based on Fechner's application of steam engine physics but not for abandoning the principle of pleasure. Pleasure is a mental experience that may accompany events and ideas, as might displeasure. Wishful thinking is an expression of the pleasure principle that may be at war with the reality principle, by which I mean what we take to be the truth. What psychoanalysis has discovered is that some sorts of discomfort and even pain can be a peculiar form of pleasure and that fearful beliefs can be adhered to against the evidence. What this book will suggest on that score is that the hidden satisfaction is in the realisation (Bion) or actualisation (Sandler) of an existing unconscious complex, or what I would call a model.

To personal sensuous satisfaction of instinct as a component of the pleasure principle and actualisation of belief I would add Trotter's "herd instinct" manifesting itself in a wish to conform and coalesce with a group belief system. This I discuss in Chapter Four. Freud's version of the reality principle, though powerful in his thinking and his dedication to natural science, is a weak concept because it is only based on an adaptation of the pleasure principle to accommodate delay. If one includes an epistemic instinct as is implicit in Klein and explicit (as K) in Bion's metapsychology, the concept is stronger and the conflict between the two principles sharper. We are to some extent truth seekers, and also pleasure seekers. Meanwhile reality as represented in science is expanding rapidly and at the same time retreating rapidly from our everyday experience of the world into unimaginable states in the subatomic quantum world and hypothesised multiverses in cosmology. What do we make the measure of reality testing in such a state of provisional and esoteric knowledge? It was ever so and surely will remain so but meanwhile we have what David Hume called his natural beliefs, that is, those he shared with others which he did not regard as logically defensible, unlike his stripped down philosophical ideas that eliminated cause and effect. It is our patients' natural beliefs that we are concerned with and we can address these with the reality and pleasure principles in mind; this is discussed in Chapter Five.

The theme of this book is that we think in models. Braithwaite, whose concept of scientific deductive systems (1953), which are essentially conceptual propositions stated in mathematical terms, suggested that we have a tendency to translate these into models before seeking confirmation of them in particular examples. I think it works differently, that we think in models first and that some people make an abstraction of this on a logical, deductive basis.

Lakoff and Johnson in their linguistic study "Metaphors We Live By" (2003) assert that metaphorical language is secondary to preverbal metaphoric structures and that metaphorical thought is ubiquitous, unavoidable, and mostly unconscious. I would call these metaphoric structures, models.

J. S. Mill (1859) took the view that belief came first and logic followed to examine it, dismiss it, or defend it. In psychoanalytic terms this would be part of reality testing, which we can subdivide as reasoning and experience. Reason, however, as we know from analytic work, can also be used to ostensibly justify and ostensibly explain unconscious beliefs held for other reasons, which we call rationalisation.

> An old argument in philosophy has been between coherence and correspondence as tests of the truth: that is by deduction and induction in the first case, or correspondence with what can be observed in the world in the second. In psychoanalysis we use both the first derived from reason, the second from experience. As Wilfred Trotter (1916) pointed out and Bion later adumbrated (1962b), human beings have difficulty learning from experience when it means changing existing beliefs.

Mathematics as an extension of logic has produced its own models and since the seventeenth century has increasingly provided an escape from our language and perceptually based models. As a result in the twentieth and twenty-first centuries we have an accurately described quantum world which we can formulate mathematically and manipulate but not imagine or adequately describe in words. From Newton onwards we have had a world modelled by mathematics, then with greater departures from our common sense world mathematics has produced quantum mechanics. It has produced another "reality", a mathematical reality: how closely the models derived from that correspond with subsequent scientific exploration of the physical world and experiment is the continuous preoccupation of modern physics.

Its great success in application means the world at large is using machinery based on physics it does not understand and that runs counter to common sense. The supreme example of which is the transistor, a beautifully realised application of quantum physics, or the magnetic resonance scanner that is another.

Meanwhile we will continue to use mental models in our natural belief systems that correspond with the old physics based on the common perceptual experiences that have been established in our brains as we evolved on our medium-sized slow-moving planet. And continue to rely on what we call common sense with its double meaning, common to all our senses and common to our fellow beings. The latter means that the "natural beliefs" of individuals is culturally sensitive; this is discussed in Chapter Five.

The title of this book is taken from a lecture I gave to open the Freud exhibition at the Science Museum in London. The first chapter is a revised and updated version of that lecture and addresses an age-old philosophical question about the relation between body and soul in its more localised contemporary form between brain and mind. I am not a philosopher nor will I be pursuing the argument by a philosophical method but speaking from the position of a practising analyst. But as William Massicote, who is a philosopher, wrote in a paper entitled "The surprising philosophical complexity of psychoanalysis (belatedly acknowledged)", "Psychoanalysis encounters virtually every philosophical problem" (1995).

Everyone approaches these questions from some personal direction: my principal interests from school onwards have been equally divided between biology and literature. I started out in general medicine and was fortunate in gaining some specialist knowledge of neurology by working as a registrar in the famous Queen Square Hospital for nervous diseases. I subsequently trained and practised in adult and child psychiatry before training in psychoanalysis, which I have practised for the last forty years. This may sound like an ascent from lower to higher, from bowels, as it were, to brain and then ascending to mind.

A jokey bit of professional jargon of my neurological days was to refer to symptoms of mental origin as "supra-tentorial". The tentorium cerebelli is a ledge of dura mater in the skull that supports the cerebral hemispheres and effectively separates them from the brain below it. The implication was clear: it was that the mind was the next level up and the supposed sufferers of non-brain based symptoms (hysterics) were referred literally "upstairs" to the "trick cyclist" (psychiatrist) on the upper floor.

Hughlings Jackson had produced a model of the central nervous system that roughly speaking had "higher functions" in the greatly expanded cerebral hemispheres above what are regarded as the evolutionary earlier and more basic brain functions. It is tempting to follow this model onwards and upwards from peripheral nerves, to brain, then to mind and even higher to spirituality. This is a good example of the beguiling character of models as Braithwaite warned us, which I discuss in Chapter Six.

Freud, writing as a neurologist in 1878, before he invented psychoanalysis, in a monograph on aphasia, quoted Hughlings Jackson's warning, "In all our studies of diseases of the nervous system we must be on our guard against the fallacy that what are physical states in lower centres fine away into psychical states in higher centres" (1891, p. 306). Higher and lower had become, thanks to Hughlings Jackson's own work, the familiar categorisation of neural activity, and so it has remained, from humble spinal reflexes through ascending levels of brain activity to the summit in the cerebrum. But as Freud pointed out in this same paper,

> Physiological events do not cease as soon as psychical ones begin; on the contrary, the physiological chain continues. What happens is simply that, after a certain point of time, each (or some) of its links has a psychical phenomenon corresponding to it. Accordingly, the psychical is a process parallel to the physiological—"a dependent concomitant". (1915 p. 207)

This latter phrase "a dependent concomitant" belongs to Hughlings Jackson.

This corresponds to the philosophical position reached by William James of "neutral monism" (as opposed to dualism) which is rather like Spinoza's view that mind and matter are different attributes of one substance, like one man known by different names, not two separate men (Russell, 1946).

It is easier for our generation to imagine this because we have a machine that resembles it. We have a mechanical model that we can use analogically, the digital computer, in which there is *hardware* and *software*. We could describe hard and soft ware as in dependent concomitance. We are always reassuringly convinced by machine analogies and then speak of "mechanisms". This excites in materialistic souls the thought we can produce a mechanical brain. If we ever do it will not be a digital brain: Penrose has suggested a quantum computer, that is something based on quantum principles not digital codes; however, a quantum computer has not yet been successfully designed, though the silicon chip is an amazing application of quantum principles. It is only a means of translating data into a digital code. There are difficulties in physics not unlike some we have in psychoanalysis. What is truly established in the world of subatomic particles does not quite mesh with large body physics and cosmology: there are difficulties in applying quantum principles in the molecular world. The elusive chemical production of life, which for so long has been rather like the ancient alchemists' efforts to transform elements, is now also being pursued by "quantum biology". A current idea is that life processes take place at the quantum edge: this is the point or on the line at which quantum principles such as super-position, probability waves, and the uncertainty principle are giving way to "decoherence". This is where "classical" rules, chemistry, random statistics, and not quantum probability (coherence) operates.

It is tempting to compare this transition to Freud's notion of the transformation from the System Ucs. (*das Unbewusste*) to the unconscious ego, from primary to secondary process: this is discussed in Chapter Two. I see it as like the transition from unconscious phantasies to unconscious belief, which is the basis of psychic reality. The ego function I refer to as the belief function precedes "reality testing".

Given my assumption that the analyst will be attempting to find the models operating in his (or her) patient's mind and to form a model in his own to correspond to it, he will need a storehouse of possible models. This accumulates from psychoanalytic learning and from previous experience. Like other disciplines there is always a search for universals, or to use a preferred phrase, "species specific" phenomena. Freud nominated the Oedipus complex as the first in his letter to Fliess in

1897. In Chapter Six I give an example of one such model learnt from Herbert Rosenfeld but I would emphasise that in many cases one is waiting for one peculiar to the particular patient to emerge.

In addition to models acquired through clinical experience, other sources include myths as in Freud's use of the Oedipus myth, and literature as in his use of Hamlet in the *The Interpretation of Dreams* (1900a). I have used Milton's *Paradise Lost* and Blake's prophetic verses in Chapter Twelve and Mary Shelley's *Frankenstein* in Chapter Eleven. Religious sources are very rich in providing models of mental life. The role can be reversed and in Chapter Nine I try to throw some light on recurrent religious wars from an understanding of internal battles between thing worship and word worship in analysis.

CHAPTER ONE

Between mind and brain

To discuss the relationship between neuroscientific studies and psychoanalytic theories we need to understand what we mean by the three words of the title: mind, brain, and between. By "brain" I do not limit it to that part of the nervous system inside the skull but all its ramifications through the central nervous system, the autonomic nervous system, and its associated hormonal activities. I do however limit the term brain to the individual's body; this boundary, however, does not apply to the mind, which I hope to show in this and the next chapter. We are so interactive we live subjectively in our relations with others both communicatively and imaginatively, attributing aspects of ourselves to others and introjecting aspects of them, and with our tribal affiliation ever present. With the aid of modern technology we can communicate at great distances, such now is the reach of our minds we can practise psychoanalysis by telephone or Skype continents apart from each other.

As a practising psychoanalyst my contribution to theories of the mind derives from exploring psychopathology, just as the contribution to neuroscience a neurologist makes is from clinical experience with neurological disorders and as physicians contribute to knowledge of physiology from its failings. So in order to show that I am not indulging in a semantic game or trying to give a philosophical account of the mind-body problem, but speaking of distinctions between clinical entities, let me refer to three cases from my own experience.

The symptomatic problem they had in common was *not being able to turn left*. The first Mr. A was a patient I met when I worked in neurology. He had a brain tumour in his parietal lobe and he suffered from "anosognosia", which in his case meant *he could not recognise the left side of his body* as his own even though it was not paralysed or insensitive, nor could he register anything to his left, nor could he complete a map that included the left side of the country. So when he left his bed he could not turn to the left. The second case, Mr. B, was a psychotic patient I had as a psychiatrist. He could not turn left because it was *wrong* as opposed to *right*: *left meant bad, right meant good*. The third case was a psychoanalytic patient of mine, Ms. C, whom I would describe as neurotic. She took a long circuitous way to my consulting room in order to avoid turning left en route because it would put her "on the wrong foot" for her oncoming session.

The first case is of anosognosia, a well-recognised symptom resulting from brain damage in the parietal region; the disorder is at the level of perceptual integration of the body image. It similarly affected his visual field and all kinds of awareness on that side of his body. His reasoning, however, was intact, his relationship to himself and his life history was normal, and one could say that although he could not relate fully to the world perceptually and operationally he was psychologically sound. My second case, Mr. B, was very much otherwise. His avoidance of turning left was aversive: the left side of the world was a dangerous, bad place whereas the right side was good. His world was divided arbitrarily in this way between good and bad. This arbitrary *splitting* is characteristic when the ordinary primal split between good and bad based on good and bad experience has failed to be realised. The term "splitting" as used in psychoanalysis describes the division of attributes, values, and qualities into segregated parts that are treated as wholes, whether this is applied to objects or the self. There are neurological reports of traumatic or surgical severance of the connections between the left and right hemispheres of the brain resulting in opposing behaviours. One such instance was described of someone getting dressed with one hand and undressed with the other. In this psychotic case, however, *the division was not at the level of perception but of value and belief*. Unlike Mr. A, the neurological case, Mr. B's relationship to the world as a whole and to himself was disturbed. Non-professional observers would have no difficulty in describing him accurately as suffering from a mental disorder; they would only be speculating if they suggested he had a brain disorder.

The last of my three patients, Ms. C, was neither deprived of normal perception as was not Mr. A, nor did she have conscious delusional beliefs, as did Mr. B. She was avoidant in her behavior and she said she was just "superstitious". *The belief underlying her superstition was that leftness was wrong and that she should not approach her analyst from the wrong side but this belief was unconscious.* So the gap in this case was between conscious and unconscious. In the first case we would talk of a brain disorder, in the second of a mental illness a psychosis, in the third of a neurosis.

This demonstrates that not only is there conscious mental life with physical brain processes underlying it, of which, like the physiological processes underlying our breathing, we are necessarily unaware, there are also "mental" processes of which we are also unconscious. By "mental" in this context I mean things which by their nature could be thought, felt, or imagined if given access to consciousness: there is, in other words, an "unconscious mind". What we regard as mental life continues to exist when we are asleep, in the form of dreams, the analysis of which can give access to already existing unconscious thoughts. Such is the familiarity with dream thinking that an experienced analyst can develop that this "royal road" to the unconscious can become idealised, as if both our patients and we ourselves are more truthful as dreamers than our waking selves. Some psychoanalytic thinkers seem to believe this as if the waking conscious mind, with its connections to the perceived world through the external senses, is inferior. This sounds to me like William Blake when preaching his solipsistic, subjectivist religion rather than when as a poet he gives expression to his relationship to life, a distinction that is explored in Chapter Eleven.

Neuroscientific theories arise from study of the nervous system and psychoanalytic theories from study of the mind: if one accepts William James "neutral monistic" view, that "there is a common substance of which matter and mind are phenomenal modifications" (Ayer & O'Grady, 1992, p. 491), the two can form a theoretical axis with concepts of brain function at one end and those of mental function at the other. They could meet in the middle in some explicable way but as yet they do not. I think we can only hope to join them up by working in detail at one end or the other. Both need to take cognisance of what is happening at the other end but not to mix them up. It is not unusual for scientific studies to be divided like this: chemistry and subatomic physics would be an example, the one studying how molecules behave, the other studying the complex subatomic particles and forces described in quantum mechanics. Similarly, mechanical engineers in order to go about their business accept as absolutes exact measurements and properties of physical materials that we know from modern physics are not what they seem but are the resultant of subatomic, very different phenomena. The same can be applied to optics for example. We know that light, in the peculiar subatomic world revealed by quantum mechanics, consists of streams of particles moving in all directions, and functioning like waves, but at the level of the optics laboratory *for all practical purposes* it moves as if it consists of calculable wave frequencies in straight lines. Mechanisms may be seen by the use of an electron microscope that remain undisclosed at the practical level of the ordinary optical microscope, yet this latter may be all that is needed for many scientific uses. But further understanding of how things really work at the atomic level in the brain are likely to be subjected to nanotechnology and the mathematical principles of quantum mechanics applied to its findings in the future of neuroscience. A nanometre is one billionth of a metre in length and the technology that enables exploration at submolecular levels is part of the growing field of quantum biology.

It seems likely that the future understanding of fundamental neural processes will lie in this direction and in parallel with this biological enquiry will be the development of quantum computers. These are yet to be developed though conceived in principle, and will be based on direct quantum phenomena unlike the digital computers, which are based on encoding data into digital sequences. However, the quantum computing though based on natural phenomena will not seem natural as it is based on concepts such as super-positions and electron entanglement which are mathematically sound and attested in practice but run counter to common sense and are counter-intuitive.

So if the physical processes of the brain are better understood by quantum biology they will not seem natural and will differ more than now from the models we develop of the e-mind. They will be much closer to the mode of operation of living cells than the current digital computer systems, which only simulate brain function by transformation into digital codes; however, this will not bring our everyday, commonsense models of thinking into line with their neural counterparts described in quantum terms. This discrepancy between our natural belief systems and the mathematical models of quantum mechanics is further discussed in later chapters.

We may need, even in the fullness of time, to apply FPP ("for all practical purposes") to our psychological approximations as compared with the nano-molecular findings of neuroscience. If, as seems likely, quantum biology reveals that the subatomic activities of the brain are governed by quantum coherence, these would be only understandable mathematically. We might have to say, FPP, the brain produces a mind but that our mainly mathematical understanding of how it does it may not mesh with our ways of thinking.

Like the linguists exploring the universal components of language, who say all language is based on physics but it's the wrong physics, we might have to say that our models of the mind are based on physics but it's the wrong physics.

Heisenberg, one of the great founders of quantum physics said:

> "Physics in the twentieth century undermined not only Classical Newtonian Physics but also common sense." He commented that, "The structure of space and time which had been defined by Newton as the basis of his mathematical description of nature … corresponded very closely to the use of the concepts space and time in daily life … Newton's definitions could be considered as the precise mathematical formulations of these common concepts. We know now", he said, "that this impression is created in daily life by the fact that the velocity of light is so very much higher than any other velocity occurring in our practical experience". (Heisenberg, 1962)

In this sense the "between" of my title may not simply be a time gap between our knowledge of mental activity and our knowledge of its counterpart in neural activity. The study of the "mind" might be a "between state" where FPP will always prevail, based on the one hand on subjective, conscious, and unconscious experience and on the other of the calculus of neural functions.

What do we mean by mind?

When we turn to the other word in my title, "mind", we move into the language of personal and social life as it has evolved as our species has evolved. The words *mind* and *mental*, in Strachey's English

Standard Edition of Freud's work, are a translation of his use of *Psyche* and *psychisch*—or *Seele* and *seelisch*—pretty well interchangeably. The word *Geist*, the usual German dictionary word for *mind* is not used. *Psyche* is Freud's use of the Greek word, a choice he also celebrates in *psychoanalysis* which he abbreviates as ψα, and when he speaks of *psychic reality*. *Seele* could have been translated literally as *soul*, which has less religious overtones in German, but it has a history in metaphysics. Strachey maintains that Freud used *Psyche* and *Seele* interchangeably so he uses *mind* for both words in his English translation. It is never the less a reminder that Freud's use of *mind* has *soul* as a precursor. The term *soul* did not drop out of English when it ceased to have a particular religious meaning. In the verse of the romantic writers of the late eighteenth and early nineteenth century such as Wordsworth, "the soul" persists and is used by him interchangeably with "mind", rather as Freud uses *Psyche* and *Seele*. For example in the ode on immortality:

> Thou, whose exterior semblance doth belie
> Thy soul's immensity. (Wordsworth, 1807, p. 300)

These lines were addressed to Coleridge, whereas in a sonnet of the same period, it is "mind" that is the essential self:

> The immortal Mind craves objects that endure:
> These cleave to it; from these it cannot roam. (1807, p. 287)

In another context, where he describes exactly what Melanie Klein would later describe as "memories in feelings" (1957, p. 180) Wordsworth says,

> … when the soul
> Remembering how she felt but what she felt
> Remembering not—retains an obscure sense
> Of possible sublimity. (1850, p. 23)

Wordsworth like Klein and Winnicott sought the explanation of the *numinous* in early infantile experience "beyond the twilight of rememberable time" as he put it (ibid.). The thread that runs through all this is that mind is successor to the soul in our language and is regarded as transcending the machine-like body because it brings aesthetic value, emotion, and imagination to the table. Equating mind simply with brain would be regarded by aesthetic enthusiasts as soulless or soul-destroying, reducing man's highest artistic achievements to products of machines such as those to be found in Blake's "dark, satanic mills". There was a time when there was a ferment of disputation between those who espoused *mechanism*, who sought the explanation of every-thing in *machine* analogies, and those who espoused *organism* as derived from *nature*. The latter regarded themselves as saving humanist val-ues from the machine, and like Coleridge warned against confusing mechanical regularity with organic form (McFarland, 1985). The heart could be regarded as a pump or as a metaphor for the source of love.

Freud began at the brain end of my imputed mind-brain axis, with mechanism in mind. His neuroscientific work led him into clinical neurology and as late as 1895 he wrote a sketch of a "Psychology for Neurologists" (1897) in neural terms. This he declared in the opening sentence was "to furnish a psychology that shall be a natural science: that is, to represent psychical process as quantitatively determined state of specifically material particles" (ibid., p. 285). This is wholeheartedly of the Helmholtz school of physiology that espoused *mechanism*, that is, sought explanation by analogy with machines, in opposition to those who favoured the use of the term *organism* who sought explanation of human functioning by natural comparisons. Freud was a considerable neuroscientist and in his project of a "Psychology for Neurologists" he intended to give an account of psychology in terms of the nervous sys-tem as consisting of the newly discovered neurons. He had, indepen-dently of Waldyer, found them from his own researches about 1891. In the project he also proposed that a great deal of their function was con-trolled at what he called contact barriers by facilitation and resistance to the passage of nerve impulses from neuron to neuron. These we now call synapses and a great deal of research and pharmacy has focused on transmission at these synapses; and much psychiatric pharmacy is based on chemical neurotransmitters. It is interesting that Freud had put his finger on this as crucial. He specified two different types of neu-ron, φ and ψ, the former freely permeable, the latter impermeable and therefore continuously charged. This distinction runs through much of his later thinking in mental rather than neuroscientific terms as in primary process and secondary process thinking. Freud also tried to give a neuronic explanation for the *ego* (*das Ich*), literally "the I", a term derived from Fichte, who was a post-Kantian philosopher certainly not of the mechanistic school. The problem Freud tried to solve in his neuronic scheme of charge, flow, and discharge was how to account for the constancy of the ego. He did so ingeniously with his theory of resistance at the contact barriers of ψ neurons. While still thinking and writing as a neurologist, writing on aphasia Freud used Hughlings Jackson's description of the relation between the mental and the physiological as parallel, that the mental was a "dependent concomitant" (1891b, p. 207).

Somewhere between 1895 and 1900 Freud abandoned this neurological project and changed ends on the brain-mind axis. At his new starting point it was not neurons but ideas that were the atoms of his inquiry and information about them came from dreams, the psychopathology of everyday life, self-analysis, literature, mythology, and most of all clinical experience. His allies now were Sophocles, Shakespeare, Goethe, other writers, and his patients. He never abandoned his conviction that psychoanalysis belonged with the natural sciences but he was now keeping company with thoroughgoing mentalists. None were more so than Fichte to whom we owe the concept of the ego. This is the starting point for the next chapter, which considers whether there is such a thing as mental causation.

CHAPTER TWO

Does the mind matter?

Descartes introduced the idea of the body functioning like a machine, and therefore spoke of mechanisms. However, he exempted what we would call mind from this, proposing the existence of a spirit which did not have any material existence. The result was what is called dualism, or Cartesianism. It is a common, unthought model in many people's minds and is taken for granted by many religions though discredited by most philosophers. Gilbert Ryle in the twentieth century satirically entitled it the "ghost in the machine". Ryle pointed out that philosophically it was a category mistake, that the mind was the totality of the thinking self, not just another part of the body; it was not just another player in a football team, it was the whole game (1949, pp. 17–19).

The opposing philosophical position to dualism is monism, that the material body and mental identity are one. This can result in a further division between those who say there is only materiality, physicalists, and those who say that there is only mentality, idealists. It is clear that psychoanalysts following Freud are monists who nevertheless accept that mind exists as a function of brain. The next question is whether anything happens as a result of mentation or is it just a by-product of brain activity? Does the mind do anything?

9

As a psychoanalyst I am convinced that beliefs can produce effects but I also believe that bodily processes can give rise to states of mind. These two propositions may sound obvious but actually not everyone believes *both* of them. Many psychiatrists believe in epiphenomenalism, a term invented by T. H. Huxley. This asserts that mental phenomena are only the accompanying experience of physically determined events: that ideas, beliefs, etc. *never* cause anything in themselves. In other words the "mind" is only a sensory organ registering the effects of physical activity produced by the body. Some psychiatric schools of thought have based themselves on that thoroughgoing physicalism; they regard mental states as accessory accompaniments of physical changes, like the bang of thunder and the flash of lightning are the perceptual accompaniment of electrical discharges and not the cause or the effect of the storm. This view lends itself to concentrating on physical treatments of mental states.

We also find others who intellectually inhabit the other end of the body-mind axis and see the physical world as just a mental construction. Absolute philosophical idealism holds that physical reality is only a creation of the mind. William Blake for example claimed, "Mental things alone are real." "Science", he said, "is the tree of death," and the eye is an organ for projection not perception (writing on "Religion and Knowledge", see Mason, 1988, pp. 3–23).

This question of the agency of the mind is built into psychoanalysis in the concept of the ego. The superego and the id are later additions to Freud's mental model but the ego has been there from the beginning. As I described in the last chapter Freud sought to account for the persistence of the ego even while he was trying out neuroscience explanations in the "project".

In order to consider the origins of that model we need to return to Fichte. He was a post-Kantian philosopher of the eighteenth/ nineteenth century who wrote "*Wissenschaftslehre*", roughly meaning a theory of science. In this he tried to reconcile how a freely, willing, morally responsible agent can be part of a world of causally conditioned material objects in space and time. He spoke of the ungrounded assertion of the subjective, spontaneity, and freedom of the "I" (*das Ich*, the ego). But he added that objective necessity and limitation were necessary conditions for the possibility of a realisation of the "I".

Fichte did not accept Descartes' definition of *cogito ergo sum*: I think therefore I am. Fichte said, "The self posits itself, and by virtue of this assertion alone it exists." I announce its existence in order to say I do anything. I am A or I = A therefore A = A. He argued that to posit I with a predicate meant I already existed, before the predicate completed it. He called it *Ichheit* (I-hood). We could say *das Ich* (the ego) is an ontological not epistemological entity. I think the corresponding notion in contemporary analysis would be Bion's concept of "O", and Lacan's comment when he reversed Descartes's aphorism, to read "I am, therefore I think."

Fichte went further, saying that this necessarily meant there was a not-I; that the assertion "I" meant that something else existed, something other. He said, "The law of consciousness: no subject no object, no object no subject" (Ayer & O'Grady, 1992, p. 134). This would correspond with Klein's view of intrinsic subject-object relations and current linguistic theory, in every potential sentence subject has an object. That the ego, as we have become accustomed to calling it, is the ultimately identifiable agency of self under the German first person singular, *das Ich*, the I. This was graphically illustrated for me in the analysis of a borderline patient. She used two different pronouns to refer to herself whilst in analysis, "she" and "me". "Me" was an anarchic boundary-less version of her self committed to the pleasure principle; "she" on the other hand was her self as a contemptible, slavish, submissive creature of conformity, "Daddy's clever, obedient, girl". The pronoun "I" was never used. When I drew attention to that the patient said, "'I' would be the chair of the board and there is no chair of the board." It was quite a long time before such a person put in an appearance in her analysis, which notably lacked a chair of the psychic board, that is, no one was in charge and no one was accountable. But in her life outside she functioned well once the analysis was established, presumably outside the transference relationship she was the "I" in her everyday dealings. That a psychotic transference within the analysis can coexist with a sane effective self outside analysis is characteristic of borderline patients. A prolonged analysis enabled her to become the psychic chair of the board which would seem to correspond to Fichte's *Ichheit*, and what Bion might have described a change in "O" not simply in "K".

Fichte spoke of different starting points in a philosophical examination, one pure selfhood (what I would call subjectivism), which would lead to *idealism*, and the other pure "thing-hood" (what I would call objectivity) which would lead to *dogmatism*. He anticipated Hegel in this essentially dialectical approach. In current psychoanalysis we meet it as in the struggle to reconcile subjectivity and objectivity. One of the difficulties in this meeting ground, under whatever names it appears, is that on both sides of the fence there is real passion. So it was in the nineteenth century with the advance of science and its machines both real and metaphoric.

Some among the nineteenth-century post-romantic proponents of soulfulness became antagonistic to mechanism and science, unlike their poetic precursors such as Coleridge and Wordsworth. Prominent among them was Thomas Carlyle, historical writer, philosopher, and pamphleteer. I was surprised to find him trying to rescue "soul" from mechanistic explanations of consciousness by relocating the soul in what he called the unconscious. He wrote, "... the principle of life" is in "the Unconscious" ... "that mystic region ... from that alone all wonders, all Poesies, and religions and Social Systems have proceeded" (McFarland, 1985, p. 192). As Thomas McFarland comments, "In this perspective, the Conscious or Mechanical is the opponent of the 'Unconscious', which surrounds itself with the aura of soul" (ibid.).

This firmly attests to an unconscious mind but its character is not that of the Freudian unconscious, yet it might be a precursor of the Jungian subconscious. Carlyle's rant against the scientific mechanists is reminiscent of Jung's letter to Sabina Spielrein against Freud's "rationalistic and materialistic" views ... "reality and the unconscious are primary ... the human being stands between two worlds. Freud's view is a sinful violation of the sacred ...". The hero (Wagner's Siegfried) unites them in a symbolic figure and harm follows if, "it is not accepted as a divine being but just a phantasy" (Britton, 2003, p. 53).

Carlyle's equation of the unconscious with the soul, thus making the personifications of the untamed mind heroically superior to those who plan or calculate, fitted with his views of individual natural supremacy, and his description of economics as the dismal science. It seems to have led him to extreme political views, such as his advocacy of the restitution of slavery in the West Indies and the abolition of democracy. He expressed and proposed ideas that seem shocking today; they did not receive political expression until the twentieth century in the form of the Nazi regime.

The soul in this period was in danger of becoming regarded as a non-biological force that elevated man in the direction of "super-man", not as an angelic spirit but a god-like creature. In current parlance it is similarly at times venerated as "creativity" when it is used not to describe productivity but as a personality attribute. In my formative years at school I was taught for good reason to beware of turning verbs or adjectives into abstract nouns and thus imagining one has discovered something that is really only a verbal invention.

By the 1880s there was an intellectual turmoil, with Helmholtz (idol of the youthful Freud) pledging that "no other forces than the common physical and chemical ones are active within the organism" (Jones, 1953, p. 45). This was in conflict with other turn of the century philosophers, such as Bergson with his *"élan vital"*, essentially a supernatural view of nature as purposive with human consciousness as the climax of evolution (Russell, 1946, pp. 714–721).

It was in the midst of these culture wars that Freud began to develop his own ideas. These culminated, shaped by his clinical experience and dream analysis, in his invention of psychoanalysis. This he firmly regarded as *a natural science of the mind*, thus bringing together the new science with the legacy of centuries of preoccupation in philosophy and literature with mental life. He was supremely equipped to do this as a gifted neuroscientist and clinician, who was familiar with classical Greek and Latin and, amazingly, the literature of Germany, England, France, Spain, and Italy.

CHAPTER THREE

Is there a system in the system Ucs.?

"In psychoanalysis there is no choice for us but to assert that mental processes are in themselves unconscious, and to liken the perception of them by means of consciousness to the perception of the external world by means of the sense organs."

—*Sigmund Freud* (1915e, p. 171)

F reud's division of unconscious mental life was into three components, a preconscious that only needed to gain attention to become conscious, a repressed unconscious containing unacceptable content, and the system Ucs. The definite article makes it clear that he thought of the last of these as a place in the mind, not simply the status of thought, conscious or not conscious, repressed or accessible to consciousness. He also makes it clear that the contents of the system Ucs. could not enter the preconscious without transformation: it was later to become *das Es* ("the it", translated as the id) (1923b). However the id is never well described, as his main preoccupation in 1923 was with the ego and superego and his new dualistic instinct theory.

In his 1915e paper Freud's "system unconscious" (system Ucs.) has no direct access to consciousness without transformation and it is as if it were naïve. It is a system of no system; rather like a political organisation dedicated to the principle and practice of anarchy, or the way molecules were envisaged as in a dynamic unstructured state in gases energised by heat. This is not a formulation of chaos but of coexistence where opposites coexist, where there are no consequences, no time or space. Once promoted to the preconscious these contents are subject to the law of contradiction, to time and place, and to necessity as described by Fichte. If you remember from the last chapter, he stated that there was a necessary confrontation of the ungrounded assertion of the subjective spontaneity and freedom of the "I" with objective necessity and limitation as a necessary condition for the possibility of the realisation of the "I". The "I" or ego is the ground on which this confrontation takes place; it is therefore the place where conflict is inevitable and psychic reality is determined. Freud in some places locates psychic reality in the system Ucs. just as he wrongly allocated reality testing to the superego briefly, but in *The Ego and the Id* (1923b) he corrected this and firmly established these as ego functions. All this, it is implied in Freud's model, takes place in the ego, and the system Ucs. remains incoherent.

This model of transition has an uncanny resemblance to the descriptions in quantum physics of the transformation that takes place when anything in the subatomic world is measured. There is what is called a "collapse of the wave function" which means that particles cannot be both waves and particles any more, nor can they be in more than one time and place, and are confined within boundaries: they are in other words now subject to the laws of "classical (Newtonian) physics". In quantum jargon quantum coherence is lost and there is a state of decoherence. The language may be confusing as decoherence is the state we are familiar with in classical physics. This is the experiential physics of life as a macroscopic body, in the astronomical slow lane, of a particular planet, earth. Classical physics certainly seems to be the physics of the ego, which, as it is that part concerned with reality testing of a mind that evolved on this planet and fitted into this planet, is not surprising.

But it is not, according to Freud the physics of the system Ucs. The psychological physics of the system Ucs. is much more fluid and he compares it with the dream work, ideas in images, condensation, displacement, mobile cathexis, and so on. This is what he called primary process as opposed to secondary process. He implies that for wordless ideas (phantasies) to make it into the preconscious they need to be married up with the elements of language, eventually "thing" presentation linked with word presentation. Freud also described the dissolution of this link in schizophrenia; he posited the loss of thing presentation in the unconscious and the paradox characteristic of schizophrenia where word presentation takes the place of thing presentation so that words became more real than things. Such a patient would regard perception of a thing as hallucination and a chosen word unchangeable reality. What can be spoken or not spoken then becomes invested with moral significance. We are reminded of religion at this point, not without reason. I will describe this further in Chapters Nine, Ten, and Eleven. Freud also cautioned himself and other metapsychologists and metaphysicians against allowing a similar process to take place when reasoning, by which abstractions become more real than phenomena.

What started out as the preconscious became described as the unconscious ego in his later 1923 model. Within this he describes the way some thoughts achieve a particular status: "When a hypercathexis of the process of thinking takes place thoughts are actually perceived as if they came from without, and are held to be true" (1923, p. 23). This corresponds to what I have described as the belief function, a process that gives the status of fact to phantasies that have originated in the system unconscious like immigrants who are given a visa and a place in the perceptual world of facts as envisaged by the ego. They only become recognised as beliefs rather than facts when the relationship of the subjective self to the idea is perceived from the third position of self observation (Britton, 1998) as described in Chapter Eight.

However, Freud wrote in a brief passage later in the paper of 1915, "If inherited mental formations exist in the human being—something analogous to instincts in animals—these constitute the nucleus of the Ucs." (p. 195). In this passage the word he used in German was *Instinkt* and not his more usual word *Trieb*, and he links these inherited mental formations to animal instinct as if implying that they are innate and initially mindless. When we use a word like mindless it hints at what should be part of the mind not finding a place within the mental apparatus. A fuller exploration of this process into mind and mindfulness became a preoccupation of Wilfred Bion in the 1960s by which time Melanie Klein's further development of her ideas on the unconscious had taken place.

The transition from system Ucs. to the preconscious I have been describing will have struck some readers as similar to Klein's concepts of the paranoid-schizoid and the depressive positions. The paranoid-schizoid position was seen as a natural precursor of the depressive position in infancy. It was described as a state where time did not exist, part objects were perceived as whole objects, identification rather than object-relating was the mode, and absolutes ruled even though other contrary absolutes coexisted. The transition to the depressive position meant integration, the perception of whole objects consisting of parts instead of part objects being seen as whole objects, a sense of time, cause, and effect, and the existence of necessity. Bion later suggested that what he called Ps and D, roughly meaning unintegration and integration, were alternating states he called Ps⟺D. I further developed this by suggesting that throughout life there are sequences of Ps⟺D as new experience is metabolised and adds to the state of development represented by n, as in for the nth time, that is the number of the sequence in a formula:

$$PS(n) \Rightarrow D(n) \Rightarrow PS(n + 1) \Rightarrow \dots D(n + 1).$$

However, the original model of paranoid-schizoid to depressive position was envisaged in infancy, what we could call $PS(1) \Rightarrow D(1)$. What Klein later described as the "deep unconscious", which she regarded as unmodified by experience, we could suggest would be part of the mind that persisted as an unconscious residue outside the cycles of $PS \Rightarrow D$. The archaic, monstrous objects of this deep unconscious Klein suggested only intruded on the ego if it was disabled by ill health as in delirium, or by traumatic circumstances, or as night terrors. The last of these she was familiar with as a not uncommon symptom from her work with children. The implication is that these eruptive figures are not "egotised" or "naturalised" but are experienced as supernatural. As I see it Klein's deep unconscious is the residue of the PS of infantile life. It is not objectless, but they are not natural objects, they are supernatural. They form the basis for beliefs about heaven and hell not normally experienced but hypothesised in religions and art, except by some individuals as visions such as Joan of Arc or William Blake.

Melanie Klein unlike Freud posits that object relations exist from the beginning of life. By doing so she populates the system Ucs. with inhabitants who need to pass through the depressive position into the ego where they might become conscious or be repressed. She saw the repressive barrier as semi-permeable allowing acceptable versions ingress by symbolism and sublimation. If, however, they were not simply repressed but split off and denied by the ego, they are not only expelled but also disowned, in political terms exiled, in theological terms anathematised: in psychoanalytic terms subjected to attributive projective identification and relocated outside the self. When this takes place part of the ego containing unacceptable thoughts is projected into others. In this way the ego cleanses itself but also depletes itself in the process.

Bion (1962b), building on the metapsychology of Freud and Klein, added other layers to these processes. The grid that he designed to help the review of current psychoanalytic clinical material also offers a graphic account of his metapsychology. The vertical axis represents in descending order the ascent from raw physiological data to psychological abstract concepts. He begins with β elements as unmentalised data requiring an alpha process (an unknown procedure) to convert them into α elements. These mentalised elements can be organised into phantasies, dreams, and models. These in turn become preconceptions which may be realised in some form of experience that converts them from imageless expectations into conceptions which I am calling models.

The beauty of this system when it is allied to his theory of innate preconceptions, what I call imageless expectations, is that it marries what Freud tentatively called "inherited mental formations" with "early experiences". Freud said of this instinctual core of the system Ucs., "There is added to them what is discarded during childhood development as unserviceable; and this need not differ in its nature from what is inherited" (1915e, p. 195).

If these "mental formations" are the "instincts" and they are preconceptions, then their realisations in object relations will have the quality of instincts; and our attachment to them, or fear of them, or hostility towards them will have instinctual force and a sense of natural rightness. There is nothing in the clinical experience of psychoanalysis more convincing than this last observation. They become what in the next chapter I will refer to as mental instincts.

So to return to the question, is there a system in the system Ucs.? I think we can say yes by taking Freud's comment that if there are inherited mental formations seriously they form the core of the unconscious. What I will be arguing is that they give rise to models that structure our thinking. Lacan's much quoted phrase, "One must set out from the notion that the unconscious is structured like a language", is very appealing. Perhaps in the light of contemporary linguistics, where there is emphasis on pre-language conceptual metaphors, one might play Lacan at his own aphoristic game, reverse it, and say that, "language is structured like the unconscious".

CHAPTER FOUR

Natural history of the mind

"Would a naturalist imagine that he had an adequate knowledge of the elephant if he had never studied the animal except through a microscope?"

—*Henri Poincaré*

I think that psychoanalysis is a natural history of the mind. Natural history is defined as "the study of living organisms in their natural habitat" (Martin & Hine, *Oxford Dictionary of Biology*, 2008, p. 433). We as psychoanalysts meet the minds of our patients in a natural habitat, that is in a human relationship. Though we do not see our patients at their homes or in the street, neither do we put them in a laboratory or subject them to experiment. In the realm of psychology we are the counterpart of naturalists, not laboratory biologists.

Natural history gave birth to biological science and remains crucial to its development. It is the continued accurate observation of living things that raises the relevant questions that laboratory science and mathematical reasoning need to address. So the precise observation of the migration of robins or salmon raises questions that lead to quantum biological explanations that biology based on classical physics failed to answer. So it might be with our mental life.

In the study of our species, homo sapiens, Wilfred Trotter made the point long ago in 1905 that the unit of natural selection, of Darwin's theory, in gregarious creatures is not the individual but the group (1916). We are a social species, like ants, bees, and many others including sheep and wolves. Consequently our minds are not produced in isolation and our mental activities are not simply the products of biological individuality. We cannot understand the organisation of bee behaviour or ant activity from a study of one of their tiny brains. For this reason they have been described as "super-organisms" (Holldobler & Wilson, 2009). The individuals are seen in such a context as like single cells in a multicellular organism, the "super–organism" of the particular hive or anthill. The counterpart to neural transmission in the brain in such a social system, whether in insects or mammals, is communication, chemical and behavioural. In homo sapiens chemical and behavioural have been dwarfed in the realm of communication by the enormous development of language. And language in the mind of individuals as well as between them.

What Trotter called the voice of the herd, psychoanalysis has enabled us to realise, are links in the internal world, where there are internal figures with which we are in communication. We can travel great distances and be apart for long periods because we believe in the continuous existence of our crucial objects and can relate to them inside our minds in their absence.

Not only do we have that recourse we have "internal object relations", models derived from external relationships and their imaginary internal versions. These models become preconceptions that seek realisation in future relationships. The transference is the most notable example and lends itself through analysis to the discovery and exploration of the preconceptual models.

As would-be psycho-naturalists we have a particular difficulty in objectively observing our own species because we are influenced by innate, unconscious impulses and responses to others that come from our social nature. From its outset psychoanalysis has had to deal with this: its founder, Freud, was an exceptional person in this regard. He was sensitive to it and yet objective about it; not so a number of his colleagues. His sense of this may have played a part in placing himself behind the couch. It certainly helps by reducing the interactive pressure to react to facial signals.

All human beings have attachments and aversions: they love, fear, and hate, and possess what redeems a great deal in analysis, curiosity.

We as social animals have beliefs and values which when they are signatories of group membership, or the glue of tribal attachment, acquire the potency of instinct. These shared totemic beliefs take precedence over what we learn from experience and form resistance to what we might learn from observation. Therein lies the difficulty: we as would-be psychological observers are subject to the natural tides of social instinct in the consulting room as well as outside it and therefore need to include these in our field of observation. Analytic neutrality, that difficult professional aspiration, does not mean freedom from emotion, it means unbiased observation of its play within ourselves. If there is any other scientific discipline that resembles this it is social anthropology, guided by the notion of participatory observation. It seems to involve being "human" while being able to see homo sapiens as one particular species among many and of seeing oneself as a specimen. Ultimately curiosity takes precedence over comfort or discomfort, approval or disapproval. It will not abolish them but it can put them in their place.

Darwin

Darwin was a great naturalist and it was his influence together with a few others that transformed amateur natural history into the professional discipline of biology. After rereading *The Origin of Species* and even more after closely studying his less often quoted book, *The Descent of Man* (1871), what has struck me is how little the radicalism of his approach has penetrated educated opinion.

Darwin, with a similar exceptional degree of detachment to that of Freud, was able to view all species, including homo sapiens, as enabled by, and limited by, their evolved, inherent, specific characteristics. His was a world view of all animal and plant species, all distinct but comparable with each other, including our own. It was not man versus the animals, it was man, homo sapiens, the animal.

As one follows his free ranging analogies from everywhere and anywhere in the plant or animal kingdom one realises just how anthropocentric we usually are: how little we see ourselves as one species among many others. For Darwin, as a naturalist, the field of observation was the organism in its own environment; in contrast, Freud's original scientific background was the physiology laboratory. For Darwin it was evolution of the organism, for Freud the search for the physiological mechanism. Freud's original unit of attention was the neuron, for Darwin it was the tribe. We owe the origin of psychoanalysis to the way Freud moved from the laboratory to the consulting room and from neurons to ideas and beliefs.

The smoke from the fire of controversy about evolution obscured the radicalism of Darwin's approach, which was to view homo sapiens as just another species, defined, limited, and located by inherent biological characteristics. This point was very strongly made by a post-Darwinian writer, Wilfred Trotter. Trotter said that the first person to point out the evolutionary significance of gregariousness in natural selection was Professor Karl Pearson. I would say the first *except Darwin himself*, who could not have been more explicit about this. Darwin made clear that essential characteristics of our species spring from the fact that we, like ants and elephants, are a social species. Like them it means we unknowingly subordinate ourselves to the group and that we have such characteristics as altruism, adherence, unconscious collectivism, and shared inherent beliefs. It follows from this that our thinking is enmeshed within an unconscious social system and we have more difficulty thinking about ourselves than we do of other species. Our membership of a herd, pack, clan, or tribe, visible or invisible, means we take as facts what are really only shared belief systems and these form a resistance against gaining knowledge that contradicts them.

So his followers who did not see this but localised the natural selection process on the individual had denied a good deal of Darwin's thinking. This has continued to the present time. In *The Origin of Species* (1859), Darwin cites the bee sting as an example of how a characteristic that has an adverse effect on the individual is preserved because it is good for the group. The bee sting has backward, serrated edges, which means the bee dies whenever it is used because it ruptures the abdomen when it attempts to remove it. It is like this because the stinger evolved from a boring instrument, the egg depositor, which was adapted to serve defensive purposes by injecting a toxin. Darwin wrote, "If on the whole the owner of stinging be useful to the community, it will fulfill all the requirements of natural selection, though it may cause the death of some few members" (p. 165). The analogy with the suicide bomber of our own species is irresistible. Darwin continually tries to persuade us to leave behind our ingrained species-specific, ethical sentiments when we study others creatures. "If we admire the truly wonderful power of scent by which the males of many insects find their females, can we admire the production for this single purpose of thousands of drones, which are utterly useless to the community for any other end, and which are ultimately slaughtered by their industrious and sterile sisters? It may be difficult but we ought to admire the savage instinctive hatred of the queen-bee, which urges her instantly to destroy the young queens ... for this undoubtedly is for the good of the community, and maternal love or maternal hatred, though the latter fortunately is most rare, is all the same to the inexorable principle of natural selection" (1860, p. 165). Poor Darwin always sounds as though, when he describes natural selection, he feels responsible for it.

> When he actually applies his ideas to our own species in *The Descent of Man* (1871) he gets even more apologetic. No wonder he waited another eleven years to publish it. "Now with the animals which live permanently in a body the social instincts are ever present and persistent," he wrote. "So it is with ourselves, even when we are quite alone, how often do we think with pleasure or pain of what others think of us ... all this follows from sympathy. A fundamental element of the social instinct" (1879, p. 136). He then adds to that the more uncomfortable, unsympathetic thoughts this engenders, but only in this footnote: Enmity or hatred seems also to be a highly persistent feeling, perhaps more so than any other that can be named. Envy is defined as hatred of another for some excellence or success; and Bacon insists "of all other affections envy is the most important and continual". Dogs are very apt to hate strange men and strange dogs, especially if they live near at hand, but do not belong to the same family, tribe or clan; this feeling would thus seem to be innate ... it would be a small step in any one to *transfer* [my italics] such feelings to any member of the same tribe if he had done him an injury and had become his enemy ... To do good in return for evil. To love your enemy ... the golden rule ... only comes with reason, instruction, and the love or fear of God .... (1879, p. 136)

In this footnote we have the essence of Darwin: in the first part he is an incredibly radical thinker. He suggests, interestingly, that the hostility behind envy originates in tribal hostility that is "transferred". What

I have called *psychic atopia*, that is, basic allergy and hence hostility to difference, he suggests might be transferred from outside the tribe to someone inside the tribe. Here is Darwin speculating long before Kleinian psychoanalysis had appeared. But in the second part of his footnote he genuflects to the sentiments of his Christian neighbours and his wife and the inculcation of the "golden rule", which runs counter to his ideas. It also illustrates how disturbed Darwin was by his own ideas as well as was his wife who thought God might damn him for them.

We can see why Darwin, living alone with his radical ideas, was so uncomfortable when they ran counter to those of his neighbours and his wife. But not, in fact, to those of his family of origin, especially his grandfather Erasmus Darwin, a notable radical, idiosyncratic thinker. Erasmus was an esteemed physician who turned down the invitation to be the king's physician. He was a naturalist, physiologist, slave trade abolitionist, and poet. His poem "The Temple of Nature" traces the progression of life from microorganisms to civilised society. His poetry, admired by Wordsworth and disliked by Coleridge, was unusual; it made references to science, botany, and steam engines.

Unlike Charles Darwin, Trotter and Pearson as belligerent followers of his ideas were not uncomfortable socially because they saw themselves as forming a group loyal to their intellectual leader. Darwin, as a radical innovator, had to wait to accumulate followers in order to have the comfort of collective thinking, as did Freud, as did Melanie Klein: both of whom have been criticised for encouraging followers. They both knew that if their ideas were going to survive they needed them. As Trotter would have it group acceptance is essential if ideas are to survive. The group does not need to be large but it does need to be identifiable. If the innovator, like Darwin, is an ordinary, socially sensitive person he/she also needs followers in order not to feel an outsider, an excommunicate.

If, however, the innovator is a socially attuned, insusceptible, "asympathetic" person there is not the same emotional need for this, as was the case of Jeremy Bentham or perhaps the most original quantum physicist Paul Dirac (Farmelo, 2009). It might be that they are free from (or lack) common sense, which is another name for axiomatic shared assumptions of our mainstream cultural group. It makes it emotionally easier for some gifted individuals to be innovative if they are also socially dysfunctional.

Bentham produced an impressive, totally logical, non-subjective, mechanically perfect, ethical and legal system that was bound to offend, and did, the common attitudes of his day. It was also liable in most individuals to produce internal conflict as it inexorably applied pragmatic judgements devoid of sympathy or empathy. It has been suggested that he suffered from Asperger's syndrome.

From how John Stuart Mill, who knew him well, described him, Bentham fitted that clinical syndrome. He was free of the constraints of the herd instinct by not being capable of joining the herd. Mill wrote of:

> ... the incompleteness of his [Bentham's] own mind as a representative of universal human nature. In many of the most natural and strongest feelings of human nature he had no sympathy; from many of its graver experiences he was altogether cut off; and the faculty by which one mind understands a mind different from itself, and throws itself into the feelings of that other mind, was denied him by his deficiency of Imagination ... Bentham's knowledge of human nature is bounded. It is wholly empirical; and the empiricism of one who has little experience. He had neither internal experience nor external ... he lived from childhood to the age of eighty five in boyish health ... he was a boy to the last. (Leavis, 1950, pp. 61–62)

Mill went on: "The feeling of moral approbation or disapprobation properly so called, either towards ourselves or our fellow creatures, he seems unaware of the existence of; and neither the word self-respect, nor the idea to which that word is appropriated, occurs even once ... in the whole of his writings" (ibid., p. 67). In the terms I am using we could say he was tone-deaf to the voice of the herd.

Trotter

Trotter was very aware of our innate tendency to cluster tribe-like around any intellectual totem and he included "Darwinism" as the scriptural basis of a new herd. "To the student of biology," he wrote, "the principles of Darwinism may acquire the principles of herd suggestion through being held by the class which he most respects, is most in contact with and has therefore acquired suggestionizing power with him" (p. 39). However, Trotter added we all need this propensity, as it is only through this that verifiable truths may acquire the potency of herd suggestion and so advance knowledge. He implied throughout his book that verifiable truth will not gain *any* ground unless it finds a way to become the voice of the herd; otherwise it is no match for its already existing unverifiable beliefs (1916).

Wilfred Trotter was possibly the first serious person in Britain to be interested in psychoanalysis; he even criticised in 1905 the new, shocking, and challenging psychology of psychoanalysis *for not being sufficiently radical*. He must have been the only person in Edwardian England to suggest that Freud was not going far enough. He was in fact one of the only two from England of the forty-two people who attended the first International Psychoanalytic Congress in Salzburg in 1908. The other British person present was his junior medical colleague and friend Ernest Jones. Trotter had already embarked on what was to become a very distinguished surgical career and it was he who drew Jones's attention to Freud's ideas. He suggested that they both learn German, which they did, in order to read Freud. They shared consulting rooms as young doctors in Harley Street, London. They also shared ideas (Maddox, 2006). One of Trotter's principal concepts has since been regarded as Jones's main original contribution to psychoanalytic theory, namely the concept of *rationalisation*. This is the production of a conscious, logical reason to justify what is an already firmly held unconscious belief. This is a cornerstone of psychoanalytic thinking and even now is a theory which is vitally important in social thinking that is not sufficiently understood. It is one of the central ideas in Trotter's original papers of "Herd Instinct and Its Bearing on the Psychology of Civilised Man", and "Sociological Applications of the Psychology of the Herd Instinct". They later formed the first two chapters of his book, *Instincts of the Herd in Peace and War* (1916).

> Another of his ideas currently achieving unacknowledged recirculation as a radical new concept goes under the title, "super organism". Trotter's notion was that the evolutionary emergence of multicellular organisms was a development of co-operation between unicellular social organisms that became co-operative cells in a new multicellular organism. In explaining what a super organism is, Holldobler and Wilson draw up a useful set of functional parallels between an organism (such as ourselves) and the superorganism that is an ant colony. The individual ants, they say,

> function like cells in our body. Many are extremely short lived. The specialised castes correspond to our organs; and the queen ant is the equivalent of our gonads. (Holldobler & Wilson, 2009)

As social animals we in evolutionary terms are like individual cells in a multicellular organism, the herd. What perhaps is particular to our species is that we have, through our capacity for imaginative identification, a means of being part of various different organic collectives through shared beliefs, as well as through kinship.

Trotter's ideas have found their way into psychoanalysis, not only his concept of rationalisation, but also through a number of the contributions of Wilfred Bion.

Francesca Bion comments in her introduction to Bion's autobiographical essay that two "outstanding" men, "played a very great part in her husband's intellectual development" (Bion, 1985, p. 7); one was H. J. Paton, a university don who was an authority on Kant's philosophy when Bion was an undergraduate at Oxford and the other was Wilfred Trotter, his surgical chief when he was a medical student at University College Hospital. If one looks for a ground where these two influences meet it is in the notion of the *a priori synthesis*.

The empirical school of philosophy following Locke claims that synthetic statements unlike analytic propositions can only be derived from experience. Kant, however, insisted that some synthetic propositions are not necessarily derived from experience; that some are inherent in the mind. William James later used this to describe a mental instinct as "an a priori synthesis of the most perfect sort" which meant that it was treated as an axiomatically obvious proposition; in other words a fact. Trotter uses James' definition to characterise those instinctive beliefs that are the manifestation of what he called the herd instinct. He emphasises, however, its plasticity in human beings; instinct does not determine the content of a particular belief but the way it is treated as a fact; it does not impose a particular ritual but it seeks to find one to express itself.

Kant claims we believe some things because of the inherent nature of the human mind; Darwin suggests that the mind has evolved the way it has because we are social animals; Trotter that the herd instinct can endow any opinion with the enormous power of instinctive belief. Trotter cites altruism as the most characteristic quality of social animals: "Man is altruistic because he must be, not because reason recommends it." But he specifies that altruism is confined within the boundaries of the psychically identified herd. He says, "Herd suggestion *opposes* any advance in altruism, and when it can executes the altruist, not of course as such but as an innovator" ...

"How constantly the dungeon, the scaffold and the cross have been the reward of the altruist" (pp. 46–47). In this instance seen as a heretic.

The altruistic innovation that incurs the wrath of the group is its extension beyond the existing boundary of identification. Its ultimate extension would seem to be currently in the human rights movement whose advocates identify as the "tribe" the whole of mankind. This as we can see soon finds itself at war with local, ethnic, national, and religious affiliations.

Yet the wish to push out beyond the boundary does also appear to be an innate characteristic of our species. It is evident as the urge to explore in both the physical world and in the realm of ideas and presumably it underlies the common tendency to "marry out". It is tempting to suggest that the sexual instinct and its derivatives are at odds with the survival instinct of the herd that always favours conservative choice. The increased size of the resulting gene pool clearly has survival value, and the greater variety of cultural expressions of our social instincts is an asset. But all of this is felt to threaten the stability of the tribe just as new ideas threaten the belief system that binds the tribe together.

Where new and old meet it seems there are two potential impulses, assimilation or annihilation. In the microcosm of individual psychology we see this conflict both in the realm of ideas and relationships. It is like a struggle between affinity and allergy. Based on my experience in analytic practice I have written about what I call a "xenocidal" impulse, the urge to annihilate that which is not self, suggesting that it is the psychic counterpart to the immune system and that some individuals are, as it were, hyperallergic to foreign ideas. The expression of this in tribal life is not hard to find. An anthropological description of 1933 made by Ernest Thesiger of the tribe the Danakil of a remote part of Ethiopia serves as an extreme example. They had a fearsome reputation in Africa because they killed strangers. Their manhood and prestige was based on the number they personally killed and a first killing was the adolescent boy's initiation rite. What is fascinating is the link between this xenophobic tribal custom and their marriage customs. They were expected to marry within the family: a man should marry his father's sister's daughter or in default, his brother's daughter

(Thesiger, 1987). Love and sex were to be legally confined within the immediate family and murder of any strangers was legitimate. Cousin marriage was axiomatic while sibling sex was taboo.

Freud was prompted by the First World War to write "Thoughts for the Times on War and Death" about the same time as Trotter's book was published. In that essay he began to entertain the idea of an innate destructive impulse in man. Freud wrote that, "[Our] loved ones are on the one hand an inner possession, components of our own ego; but on the other hand they are partly strangers, even enemies. With the exception of only a very few situations, there adheres to the tenderest and most intimate of our love-relations a small portion of hostility which can excite an unconscious death wish" (1915b). Later in his paper on *Group Psychology and the Analysis of the Ego* he took this further and linked it to his new concept of the death instinct. He wrote:

> When this hostility is directed against people who are otherwise loved, we describe it as ambivalence of feeling: and we explain the fact, in what is probably far too rational a manner, by means of the numerous occasions for conflicts of interest which arise precisely in such intimate relations. In the undisguised antipathies and aversions, which people feel towards strangers, with whom they have to do we may recognize the expressions of self-love—of narcissism. This self-love works for the preservation of the individual, and behaves as though the occurrence of any divergence from his own particular lines of development involved a criticism of them and a demand for their alteration. We do not know why such sensitiveness should have been directed to just these details of differentiation; but it is unmistakable that in this whole connection men give evidence of a readiness for hatred and aggressiveness, the source of which is unknown, and to which one is tempted to ascribe an elementary character. (1921c, p. 102)

If we view ourselves as programmed by natural selection as social animals the source of this xenocidal impulse does not seem to be so obscure. It is just as much an innate characteristic of our species as other characteristics arising from our gregarious nature that we prefer to regard as virtuous, such as altruism, self-sacrifice, worship, and obedience. Despite his reluctance to see group psychology as more than an extension of individual psychology, Freud's development of the concept of the superego provides us with a perfect inner representative of the voice of the herd. What expresses more forcibly the dread of exile or anathematisation than his words, "To the ego, therefore, living means the same as being loved—being loved by the super-ego ..." (1923b, p. 58).

Our psychoanalytic practice has provided us with ideas that can throw light on the deployment of these social instincts in individual life. Principal among these are transference and identification; we nominate our basic herd to which we owe allegiance by identification and we locate the authoritative voice of the herd by transference, and we through transference also locate the identity of the predator. In the first case we call it positive transference, in the second negative transference: both may play their part in analysis. Transference is not limited to the analytic consulting room; it shapes the emotional life outside it. It is customary in psychoanalytic theorising to derive the current transference from the family relationships of the past. I would suggest that these family relationships were themselves in a sense transference relationships by which I mean the family was the locus for the expression of our innate social instincts. As life moves on that location can change and the voice of the herd may be relocated but wherever it resides it loses none of its power. If it finds itself located in the doctor it produces the placebo effect, if in the therapist a transference cure. In a world where cures are hard to come by it might seem churlish to dismiss these; the reason for doing so, as Freud did, is their transitoriness. If transference cures develop a religious nature and they become more entrenched in a cult that is perhaps our counterpart of the beehive.

Belief revisited

It seems that as a species we are good at finding things out but not at accepting what we find, good at science but not much good at accepting its conclusions. From practising psychoanalysis and from submitting to it ourselves we can corroborate that statement. In the microcosm of analysis we recurrently encounter facts about ourselves and our personal world that should change our beliefs but they do not. An analysis in which unconscious belief is revealed in such a way to allow it to be rebutted by experience is not usually the end of the story, though now conscious and in conflict with other firmly held beliefs or known facts it is likely to persist.

As a patient put it to me in exasperation, "Though I leave here for the umpteenth time knowing how fruitless it will be to agree to do what I know to be impossible I no sooner reach home than I do so." He added, "It is not that I feel persuaded to do it I believe myself that I must do it."

This I saw as the reassertion of a belief discredited, overturned but not relinquished. I wrote about beliefs being like object relations and their actual relinquishment requiring a period of mourning (Britton, 1998). Rereading Trotter I can see that abandoning a belief that has acquired instinctive status, that is, one that unconsciously binds the individual to the representative on earth of his incorporeal tribe, means encountering the dread of isolation.

Isolation, and excommunication for an ordinary member of a social species, is the same as death. For the ego not to be loved by the super-ego, or God, is the same as death. Not to be loved by the internal representation of the tribe, clan, religious sect, fellow members, is the same as death.

I had a patient, Mr. D, who could not understand the acute states of dread he experienced, amounting to terror at times, when his mind changed and he actually accepted fully what he claimed he already believed!

Mr. D was a successful artist who worked with a woman agent and studio owner whom he now realised was grossly financially exploiting him based on unrealistic expectations of phenomenal success. Having achieved modest success he was no longer dependent on his business partner's support and had offers from other studios as he was widely accepted. But the truth of this was only available to him when he was talking in his analytic sessions.

When he returned to his partner he no longer believed this to be the case and joined her in planning future ventures, with real conviction, to his own considerable financial disadvantage. His mistrust of his partner returned fully when he next talked to me in his analytic session. Her enthusiasm for his work initially had been very important to him and she had shared with him her grandiose ideas of his future as a great artist.

We had linked this to his childhood when his mother believed he was a genius and was going to have the great artistic success she believed she was entitled to but had been denied by marrying. In fact she did not work and depended on her reliable, financially successful husband whom she denigrated. My patient only had relief from his mother's dictatorial possessive claims on his supposed genius from his pragmatic, kindly father who was mainly obliterated.

His change of mind meant he now believed a psychic reality he had previously resisted was felt by him unconsciously as turning a deaf ear to the unspoken voice of the pack leader. He feared this would in some way lead to his discredit and professional extermination. The cupola of the analytic transference, like his relation to his father, provided a temporary shelter that allowed a change of mind in the sessions, but for a long time it did not extend its effects beyond the boundary of the consulting room.

My interpretation of his situation was: "We now know that fundamentally you believe X your partner *must* be trusted. In this you may be right or not. What you need to know is that you believed it once passionately, now desperately, and that means you will very likely continue to believe it whether it is true or not. You may also believe that to doubt X means you face the disaster of psychological exile." On this basis enlightenment consists of achieving a sceptical position in relation to our own beliefs as well as other people's. I have described this as the third position (Britton, 1989).

Neutral scepticism is central to psychoanalysis as it is to all natural sciences, and it provides us with a new tribe, our fellow scientific sceptics. This collective identity protects us from the need to submit to the belief system of the larger group we call public opinion. This scientific, sceptical collective also needs a basic tribal belief to feel sane and secure. This basis of scientific belief seems to be that the truth is only ever provisionally known. In absolute terms it is always just out of sight over the horizon; the hope is that we are travelling towards it. But the crucial fact is that it exists and is independent of, and will survive, all our misunderstandings. This admirable professional position can be developed and sustained when we are at work.

We cannot live comfortably, however, without our *natural beliefs and sensibilities*, which we could call prejudices, unless like Jeremy Bentham we float through life unmoored by intuitive connections, without psychic intimacy, and free of assumptive ethical bearings.

CHAPTER FIVE

Natural, unnatural, and supernatural beliefs

I have taken the term *natural* from David Hume's description of those beliefs by which he lived outside his study in contrast to those that resulted from his rigorous philosophical analysis whilst in it. As A. J. Ayer put it, "Like the rest of us, he allowed himself to be guided in the practical conduct of his life by what he called *his natural beliefs*, but he did not claim that this was rational" (1973, p. 140). *Natural* has been for a very long time a virtuous word and in philosophical, religious, and political discourse there has long been a wish to claim it. St. Thomas Aquinas in the thirteenth century laboured philosophically to justify his Christian beliefs as natural theology and his ethics as natural law. Similarly many Muslim teachers currently seek to justify Sharia law as natural law. Natural beliefs are regarded as *selbstverständlich*, self-evident facts; William James described them as mental instincts. The adjective natural is always virtuous: it not only justifies a belief it sanctifies it.

Ever since Darwin it has had even more force: natural selection has meant that fumbling nature rather than divine precision has shaped who we are. Physics in the twentieth century paralleled the biological revolution of the nineteenth century by overturning Newtonian classical physics with quantum mechanics: replacing precise determinism with probability, and Newton's laws of mechanics with the uncertainty principle. This undermined not only classical physics but also common sense. Heisenberg commented that, "The structure of space and time which had been defined by Newton as the basis of his mathematical description of nature ... corresponded very closely to the use of the concepts space and time in daily life ... Newton's definitions could be considered as the precise mathematical formulations of these common concepts ... we know now that this impression is created in daily life by the fact that the velocity of light is so very much higher than any other velocity occurring in practical experience" (1958). In other words our natural, scientific beliefs evolved as we have evolved, relating to large objects on our relatively slow moving, moderately heated planet. Thanks to natural selection our brain is equipped to address the mechanics of a molecular world not a quantum world, so we should not expect to find its mathematical descriptions of subatomic particles seem sensible just because we can calculate their workings. But if was not for the limitations imposed on our minds by our adaptation to the macroscopic world we live in, we would not be able to think at all.

In the subatomic sphere experiments and applications have been catching up with mathematically based theoretical models. Physicists have pointed out that since Newton and others such as Leibnitz there has been another version of reality, mathematics. It has created a system of invention that only relies on its own principles and internal coherence. Science starting with Newton has been trying to catch up to examine how well the mathematical models match up with models based on physical observation. Where this proves to be impossible, at least at present as in cosmology, mathematically fuelled imaginative models emerge. It is notable to a psychoanalyst that these have the look of symbolic versions of biologically based phantasy. For example the speculative theories about multiverses, multiple numbers of universes, include one called cosmological natural selection proposed by Smelling (2013). This posits that new universes are born inside black holes that in turn spawn more black holes in their newly formed universes. Thus our universe would have ancestry and progeny. The core tenet is "Every black hole in our universe is the seed of a new universe." This results from the hypothesis that quantum gravity does away with singularity, that is, a beginning and an end. Singularity has a religious ring to it: "I am Alpha and Omega, the beginning and the ending, saith the Lord" (Revelation I v.8). The arguments for and against these propositions are mathematical but it is the models that grip the mind. It is as if they represent a battle for the mind between theology and biology: might one say superego and the word versus ego and the womb?

It is interesting that at this juncture in cosmological research and theorising biological models are reasserting themselves. I would suggest that where physical confirmation of mathematical models is unobtainable, imaginary models fill the space based on psychological models. Just as in personal life where there is an absent object and a dark area of ignorance or uncertainty, pre-existing complexes fill the mental space with imaginary scenarios. It is part of the technique of psychoanalysis to create these in order to see what emerges in the way of overdetermined personal complexes in our patients. Thus as time has passed interpretations about analytic breaks have increased.

These twentieth-century scientific developments enlarged the gap that Hume had indicated exists between the outcome of rigorous analytic work and the necessary basic assumptions of daily life. It is the latter that we live by and on which we stand because our capacity to have natural beliefs is a result of the evolution of our species. What those natural beliefs are is another matter: obviously they are culturally permeable and they change over time; they also evolve and some of us may say they also sometimes regress.

When archaic beliefs make a reappearance they are regarded as unnatural. In Freud's account in his paper on "The 'Uncanny'" he suggests that the startling, scary experiences that can arise from some misperception are because they reactivate an archaic belief. He used the word "*unheimlich*". This was translated as "uncanny" by Strachey. I think the German *unheimlich* complements more what I mean by unnatural.

"Eating people is wrong" was reiterated as an ethical baseline of a borderline patient of mine who could not find any set of rules persuasive enough to require her consent. She was in the business of trying to repudiate the natural beliefs of her parents but even she would have described the belief of Armin Meiwes as unnatural. He was found guilty of the murder and cannibalism of Bernd Brandes. Meiwes happily admitted that he had advertised for a volunteer on the internet and had killed him, chopped him up, and eaten him, thus fulfilling a fantasy he had entertained since his father died when he was a child. Meiwes's comments perfectly illustrate Karl Abraham's analytic ideas about psychic incorporation (1908). "With every bite," Meiwes said, "my memory of him grew stronger ..." Since eating Brandes he felt much better and more stable. "Brandes spoke good English," he said, "and since eating him my English has greatly improved." This illustrates Abraham's notion of our unconscious cannibalistic phantasies and incorporation, but when they surface as a conscious belief we all would regard it as unnatural: perhaps even more so Brandes's apparent readiness to be eaten and incorporated. These beliefs we see as individually idiosyncratic and therefore as manifest psychopathology, though accepting them as possibly universal unconscious phantasies. An analyst whose work I was supervising described the dream her patient brought to a session. In it he was sitting with her on a couch and together they were carving up and eating a human body. Though the symbolic meaning was clear to her she shuddered and felt unnerved when she heard it. The patient recounted his dream with the same sangfroid in the session as in the dream. Later she interpreted to him that he projected his horror into her. He, however, responded by saying "Why horror? It's only natural." It is the relation to beliefs that make them natural or not rather than the beliefs themselves. In individual psychology as in this patient it is the relationship to what might be universal unconscious phantasies that is crucial.

Similarly the natural beliefs of one culture seem unnatural to another. Female circumcision remains the prevalent practice in the rural areas of Egypt despite the fact that it is illegal and that intensive education programmes have been instituted. Those women who practise it and all those who advocate it regard it as natural. Until there is a change in the belief system the practice will remain.

David Hume recognised that he was fortunate to be able to return to his natural beliefs when leaving his study. He wrote, "Most fortunately it happens, that since reason is incapable of dispelling these clouds, nature herself suffices to that purpose, and cures me of this melancholy and delirium ... I dine, I play a game of backgammon, I converse, and am merry with my friends; and ... after three or four hours' amusement ... these speculations appear cold, and strained and ridiculous ... Here then I find myself absolutely and necessarily determined to live. And talk and act like other people in the common affairs of life."

One patient of mine, Miss A, was not so fortunate. She lacked David Hume's capacity for natural beliefs and lived every day in a nightmare cognitive world such as he described philosophically. Miss A had no basic assumptions of continuity of the sun, the moon, her mother, her brother; continuity was a daily crisis. Similarly *probability* did not exist for her, only *possibilities*. Unless, therefore, she could convince herself of her love object's exact whereabouts she was in a panic. Her ultimate weapon against uncertainty was a system of counter-beliefs, which she then treated as knowledge. One such unnatural belief was that she would go blind if she did not see her mother. From childhood her greatest fear was the fate of her mother when she was *out of sight*. Her mother's continuing existence *out of sight* meant she was *in the other room*. The *other room* was her parent's bedroom, the setting of the primal scene. My patient only thought of this as a murderous scenario. She believed her father's sex with her mother was murderous rape. Her counter-belief to her idea that her mother was being murdered was that she was not out of sight but that she herself was blind. This was reiterated like a chant: "Unless I see my mother I will go blind."

The only method of ridding herself of her doubting thoughts was to take a number of physical actions that evacuated her mind, such as repeatedly flushing the toilet. Another method was to wash her hair compulsively. When her fears that she would go blind if she did not see me became part of the transference she recruited the supernatural. She was Jewish but had no formal religious belief, but as I eventually discovered she helped herself to a Roman Catholic solution to my absence between sessions. She carried a small bottle which she filled from the tap in my bathroom at the end of each session and used this holy water to anoint herself in the intervals.

Miss A's unnatural ideas about the sun and moon were very like the cosmology of the ancient Egyptians. As the sun god's boat sailed through the underworld of dark night in order to reappear next morning, the chaos monster threatened its passage. "In every access of darkness—in an eclipse, in the waning of the moon, in a cloudy sky but above all at the onset and end of the night—Apophis the chaos monster was at work" (Cohn, 1993, p. 21).

If Miss A lived in a world much like the one Hume described philosophically, my second patient, Dr. B, lived in one like that ruled over by that forerunner of quantum thinking, the Red Queen in *Alice Through the Looking Glass*. There one could believe three impossible things before breakfast, and memory recalled things that had not yet happened so people were tried for offences they had not yet committed.

Like Miss A, Dr. B lacked basic assumptions but unlike her he was not persecuted by his lack of natural beliefs. His complaint was that his life lacked substance and the world lacked significance.

Normally, I think, a sense that the physical world has *significance* comes from its investment with *psychic reality* by projection. In a complementary way a sense of internal *substance* derives from the reintrojection of the psychic qualities with which we endow our external objects. Projection and reintrojection is a continuous cyclical process in life and is manifest in the interplay between patient and analyst. With Dr. B this flow of traffic was stopped and something else was substituted for it.

This had the characteristic of alternation, but was not dynamic: it corresponded to what Bion termed "reversible perspective" (1962b, p. 58). Bion took his term from those pictures in which foreground and background are reversible so that two different images, a vase or two facial profiles, can be perceived as alternative possibilities. This Bion thought was what was obtained in some analyses, when whichever end of the subject-object pole the analyst selected the patient took the other: thus they could alternate positions while remaining in basically the same situation. The one perspective was simply the inverse reciprocal of the other. I described it as "negative, or inverse, symmetry". There was no ultimate outcome and therefore no consequences. No firm belief was established that was not immediately reversible.

Dr. B's dreams were repeatedly of parallel lines. He had dream images that illustrated our transference relationship: for example, two men in one shirt with one arm each in each sleeve. In another dream he and his mother were driving a car, each with a hand on either side of the steering wheel. Alternating with this was another car that had the same arrangement but in this it was with his father.

Dr. B was the oldest of three children and the birth of his two sisters came as a great shock to him. He was eight years old when his second sister was born. During his mother's pregnancy he suffered an unusual symptom: he developed intermittent micropsia. He would wake in the night to find that everything in his room had become tiny. This frightened him considerably but he did not disclose it to anyone. Charles Dodgson and Jonathan Swift had this symptom.

When he first came to analysis Dr. B virtually had no childhood memories but made a few fixed statements about the past, which were invariant; his accounts of them were always couched in the same phrases. One such statement was that his parents lived in the same house but on different floors, throughout his childhood. This served to structure his phantasy that he was involved with each parent separately. In all his phantasies the positive and negative versions of the Oedipus complex were treated as reversible, inverse parallels which would never converge.

In a dream Dr. B had gone to his male dentist's office where he met an attractive woman receptionist with whom he began a sexual relationship. The scene changed in the dream and he found himself on the analytic couch where he was lying between the woman and myself. Our heads were at opposite ends of the couch. So Dr. B had to oscillate from one position to the other between the two figures and this oscillation had the quality of a sexual experience.

This insertion of Dr. B into the primal scene so that his oscillation took over the parents' sexual movements dismantled the primal scene and its triangularity, substituting parallel inverse relationships of his two relationships. By this means he formed a half identity in projective identification with one object and another with its negative.

By using negation in forming a parallel link there was always silent opposition to every agreement. This inverse symmetry provided "balance" as an alternative to integration. This also applied to belief: the state of both knowing and not knowing something, which Freud called disavowal, protected him from the emotional consequences of real belief by treating them as a pattern of inverse symmetry. In this way what is known is not consequential because it lacks the continuous adherence provided by the glue of natural belief.

It was evident that my patient treated crucial asymmetric antitheses as if they were simply *symmetrical* inversions. So true/false, love/hate, child/adult, psychic/material were exchangeable with up/down, left/right, front/back, clockwise/anticlockwise, which are symmetrical inversions.

He had a phantasy of himself as having two skin surfaces, one facing outwards and one facing inwards as if he lived between them. He dreamt of a live baboon that could turn itself inside out. Such was the structure of this psychic organisation that two worlds were simply antitheses of each other like two sides of a mirror. Categorical distinctions between such things as right or wrong, true or false, were treated as proliferating paired opposites like right and left, up and down, or north and south. Fact and fiction were similarly treated as inverse symmetries. His perceptions were often treated as reversibly interchangeable with ideas that contradicted them as if they had the same claim on his belief. In his dreams top became bottom; right became left; north of the river became south of the river. In one dream of playing the piano the bass became the treble and the white notes became the black notes. In this symmetrical universe subject and object were interchangeable in which the geometry was based on parallel lines and there were no triangles.

Conclusion

If I can summarise what I have been saying it is that we live within kinship groups in which our familial bonds are shared beliefs. These we regard as common sense in both senses of the word, and manifestly ethical. Our natural at home beliefs we contrast with unnatural, *unheimlich* beliefs. Archaic beliefs and those of cultures alien to our own we regard as unnatural, for example cannibalism, female circumcision, and suicide bombing. A great deal of unconscious phantasy is thought to be unnatural if it achieves the status of belief in individuals, and beliefs seem natural when we share them with significantly designated others.

However, a great deal of modern science is not included amongst our homely, everyday beliefs and until it is it does not gain general acceptance. What appears to happen is that a scientific culture is then established with its own local natural beliefs. We, in the analytic community, all belong to one that began at the beginning of the twentieth century and as in all communities there are boundary issues.

Trotter suggests that when a scientific group forms around an innovator his ideas are felt to be natural by his followers who are spared the isolation and anxieties of their originator. The Darwinians of Trotter's generation already included his theories in their assumptive world and took his shockingly innovative ideas as self-evident and were spared his anguish and isolation.

This movement from disintegrative innovation to established beliefs will strike some of you as resembling Kuhn's ideas on scientific revolutions (1962). Kuhn's paradigms are like natural beliefs and the collapse of the paradigm through accumulated anomalies leads to post-paradigm states of painful confusion. Bion's alternation of PS and D is similar and following Klein and Bion I expressed it as movement from Dn, as the integrated part of a recurrent cycle with PS(n + 1) as the disintegrated state that follows it.

If such a process is recurrent how does science advance? Here I think the ideas of a great nineteenth-century mathematician, Henri Poincaré can help. He proposed that mathematicians only produce new solutions to unresolved problems by intuitively selecting one fact from the very many confronting them. This selected fact re-patterns not only the current facts around but also pre-existing known facts. Bion adopted this model and applied it to our efforts to achieve analytic understanding through the intuitively selected fact. There is a problem in applying this, on which John Steiner and I wrote a joint paper. Given the power of natural beliefs, that is, the already existing theories, overvalued ideas can function as selected facts and overvalued ideas are what come naturally. So our struggle is to free ourselves from the comforting embrace of our ostensible established certainties whilst in our consulting rooms. This Bion advocated by the conscious effort to free ourselves of memory and desire in preparation for a session, in order to achieve what Freud called free floating attention. It is a sort of freedom only achieved through rigour or relaxation through effort.

What I would join David Hume in emphasising is that when the day is done we should feel entitled to leave our consulting rooms and return to the comfort of our unjustified, natural beliefs at home, while regarding them with unarticulated scepticism as nothing more than a pair of comfortingly familiar mental slippers.

CHAPTER SIX

Models of the mind and models in the mind

"In the absence of a paradigm ... all of the facts that could possibly pertain to development of a given science are likely to seem equally relevant. As a result early fact-gathering is a far more nearly random activity than the one that subsequent scientific development makes familiar."

—*Thomas S. Kuhn* (1962, p. 15)

In a small cottage in the tiny village of Grasmere in Cumbria in 1802, a "circle" consisting of William, Dorothy, and John Wordsworth, Samuel Coleridge, and the Hutchinson sisters Martha and Sara described what they were doing as lighting a lantern to illuminate the whole world. What they were in fact doing was writing poetry, making commentaries, talking, reading, and discussing with each other while living frugally. They described it as plain living and high thinking: they were inventing a model.

Clearly they thought that they were not only producing literature they were setting an example to the world on how to live. The implication of the language, with its implicit polemic, is that it contrasts with luxurious living and low thinking. It was their *model* of the good life.

They thought that if others followed it the world would be a better place. One could see them as the "hippies" of their day, or as high-minded, secular worshippers of nature. They added to their love of nature, detailed observation, introspection, and hard thinking. As in some religious precedents they prescribe a strong diet of ideas for the mind while purifying the body by curbing indulgence.

As I describe it in a tangle of metaphor it is nevertheless the basis of a model. These days it would be called a "lifestyle", a term that is metaphoric, using dressing up to describe a way of life. Wearing ideas like clothes implies they can be in fashion and out of fashion and they can be taken off or put on.

In all these examples metaphors serve as models. In many discussions the assumption is made that an original proposition is logical and clear of imagery and that the trope is rhetorical. But if we look more closely as psychoanalysts we see that the original meaning is derived from the metaphor and not the other way round; we register this by describing these as symbolic figurations. For example, a patient begins a session by describing how she is unable to park her car as usual since a new arrival in the street has taken that space. I link this with her recent complaint on discovering the existence of a new fellow patient. This is linked to memories of the arrival of a younger sibling. The model then appears in an endless variety of metaphoric tropes, such as the new girl at the office, a new rival publication, a new system of accounting, and in various guises in her dreams. Whichever way it does it, a model has been delineated that will thereafter be in her analysis in a variety of past, current, and future situations. If, as Hanna Segal described, the patient has not completed the process of symbolisation, a symbolic equation now exists in which the symbolic situation will be treated as a singular factual situation and the patient will not have sibling problems but parking problems.

What grammarians might call metaphors or even allegories Bion describes as transformations and he suggests that it is by these that we not only comprehend the configuration of our ideas but it is through them that we repeat them. Here he links with Freud's idea on repetition as transformation of an ideational complex into some form of action.

I am suggesting that we think initially and inescapably in models, whether as scientists, psychoanalysts, patients, or babies. I am asserting that we think in models, whether we are conscious of it or not, and when we believe that we are dealing directly and only with facts or theories we are probably in the grip of an unacknowledged model. Thinking in models has enormous advantages for us as a species, in representing the unknowable world in a form in which we can locate ourselves and with which we can engage. But it also has disadvantages for us whether as natural scientists, psychoanalytic theorists, practising analysts, or simply as individuals. We can become in Wittgenstein's phrase the fly in the "fly bottle" of our own model, with its own language from which philosophy might have a part to play in rescuing us.

The baby and the bath water

From my youth onwards, whenever I contemplate revising ideas I think of the phrase drummed into me, "Don't throw out the baby with the bath water." Brewer, in his *Dictionary of Phrase and Fable*, tells us "throwing the baby out with the bath water [means] overzealous reform, reorganisation or action which in getting rid of unwanted elements casts away the essentials as well" (Evans, 1970). I started this book thinking about psychoanalytic theory in this way: how do we get rid of unwanted elements while keeping essentials and then can we agree on what are the essentials? Can we agree which is baby and which is bath water? To give an example: the eighteenth-century Enlightenment cognoscenti, according to their intellectual successors in the "Romantic movement", discarded the cloudy waters of irrationality and supernaturalism but threw out the baby of human experience and imagination when doing so.

To take another example, we can ask, did Wittgenstein throw out the baby of philosophy when he threw out the bath water of philosophical discourse? In Wittgenstein mark II he repudiated not only Wittgenstein mark I but also all "the bewitchments of philosophical theories", which he thought blinded us to actual language (Pears, 1971, p. 16). Indeed, he was inclined to suggest to his followers that they should give up philosophy and do something useful. Was Bion tempted, when he had his "second thoughts" about the bath water of his earlier papers, to ditch the baby at the heart of Kleinian theory? Actually what he did, I think, was to put the baby back in the bath water with his theory of the container and the contained.

As I suggested, I started this paper thinking about psychoanalytic theories and thought I had adopted this familiar aphorism to illuminate it. But when I started associating to my metaphor I found myself recollecting early infantile memories and at the same time looking at psychoanalytic theory in the form of a model of a psychoanalytic baby in an environmental bath. Theory one, commonly attributed to "the Kleinians", concentrates on what the baby is like; so we have a variable baby in standard bath water. In contrast, and opposition to this, we have some followers of Winnicott who concentrate on the environment; so we have a standard baby and variable bath water. Bion offers us a model of variable babies in variable bath water, which he called the container and the contained. For some followers of Melanie Klein, such as Esther Bick, observing real babies in real baths seemed to offer the only useful information. Others such as Hanna Segal and Betty Joseph countered that this no doubt added to our knowledge about development but can never answer what goes on in the baby's mind that turns up later in analysis. So they said, let us limit our ideas to what we find in the current psychoanalytic process. This gives us another model, a virtual baby in a virtual bath.

You may well say, never mind these associations, what is going on here in this chapter? What is going on is me trying to illustrate what Freud called "overdetermination" which I believe applies not just to our dreams or symptoms but also to our theoretical models and clinical practice. What I am suggesting is that our mental models, shaped by personal recollection, particular desires, or fondly favoured theoretical constructions are likely to be overdetermined and tenaciously held.

You will have noticed, however, that I am discussing models as it were from two opposite ends of human mental function. At one end we have ourselves as scientific psychoanalysts, producing models to facilitate theory making, and at the other end ourselves as individuals from infancy onwards unknowingly using them in order to think at all. Since the seventeenth century, poetry and philosophy have been looking at these two ends as objectivity and subjectivity. One place where these two ends meet is in the psychoanalytic consulting room, where we are trying to discern the models that already inhabit our patients' minds and where we also bring our theoretical models.

Bion, who addressed the questions that arise at this interface, emphasised that the analyst's potential theoretical model should act as a container for the patient's personal model and not the other way round. In other words that the patient's state of mind should find a home in an appropriate model in the analyst's receptive mind and *not* an analytic model looking for a container in a patient, like a theory looking for an example to give it substance.

Freud from the outset did, as a neuroscientist, make mental models such as the *Project for a Scientific Psychology* (1950a) and at the same time he discerned what he thought were ubiquitous internal models, with personal variations, within his patients. The latter he called complexes, notably the Oedipus complex. Actually if we look at the Oedipus myth from which he derived this we can find a number of other models: one such is described in the next chapter. Through mythical, biblical stories, fairy stories, and other literary sources we can arm ourselves with a large store of models in addition to those produced for us by our professional forebears and our psychoanalytic colleagues. We may find that this tallies with what emerges from our patients, enabling us to fit the patient's subjective mental model into a theoretical frame so that we can fill out the gaps in the patient's schema. Beyond all this we find in some patients an underlying skeletal script that manifests itself in repeated patterns in different places and times with no apparent linkage other than analogy; in these we can, eventually, recognise an underlying model that may be particular to that patient.

Models in science, linguistics, and psychoanalysis

We who practise analysis know that much of our work is associative and analogical, not experimental or logical. It has led to accusations of it being not only unscientific but also counter-scientific. I think at this point in the development of science in general, and neuroscience and linguistics in particular, we can stop apologising.

Gerald Edelman, whose work on the development of the immune system earned him the Nobel Prize, has suggested that the brain develops in a way analogically similar to the immune system. Writing on brain development and function he says,

> The notion of re-entry as essential for brain development and function puts the emphasis not just on action but also on inter-action of brain areas. In a selectional brain, memory, imaging, and thought itself all depend on the brain "speaking to itself" by re-entry. Brains operate primarily not by logic but rather by pattern recognition ... it is likely that early human thought proceeded by metaphor ... The metaphorical capacity of linking disparate entities

derives from the associative properties of a re-entrant degenerate system. (2006, pp. 57–58)

Stephen Pinker, reviewing current linguistic theory, says, "I think that metaphor really is a key to explaining thought and language" (2007, p. 276). Lakoff and Johnson in their linguistic study *Metaphors We Live By* assert that metaphors are fundamentally conceptual in nature: that metaphorical language is secondary to preverbal metaphoric structures; and that conceptual metaphors are grounded in everyday experience. They say metaphorical thought is ubiquitous, unavoidable, and mostly unconscious. We live our lives, they say, "on the basis of inferences we derive from metaphor" (1980).

What Lakoff and Johnson and other "post-Chomsky" linguists call structural metaphors I am calling models and these models are based on object relations. The linguists are saying that language is patterned on pre-existing conceptual models and not the other way round: that universal basic grammar that underlies all actual human languages is species specific and innate. This corresponds well with Bion's notion of preconceptions. So my model baby, for example, grasped that being in bath water was different from being bath water well before he could speak, and long before he learned words like inside and outside.

In the twentieth century there were parallel developments in theoretical physics, in philosophy, and in psychoanalysis, and recognition that in order to theorise models were necessary. A definition from physics will clarify this: "A model is a simplified description of a physical system intended to capture the essential aspects of the system in a sufficiently simple form to enable the mathematics to be solved … some models require approximation techniques … later when exact solutions are available they can be used to examine the validity of the model" (Isaacs, Daintith, & Martin, *Concise Science Dictionary*, 1996). In chemistry models of energy storage and release were made, such as Krebs's cycle; in biology the DNA model opened doors in genetics. In physics the mathematical models of quantum mechanics transcended the time/space concepts of classical physics, which proved inadequate to describe subatomic particulate matter and the movement of particles. In turn quantum provided its own models and principles that provide mathematical understanding but which contradict common sense and the unformulated physics of our basic grammar.

Bion's thinking on models was considerably influenced by R. B. Braithwaite: he was a philosopher of science who was an important member of the Wittgenstein circle. Braithwaite examined the nature of scientific explanation, and described "scientific deductive systems" (SDS) in mathematical terms (1953). These general systems could only be tested in specific instances derived from them. However, specific instances can only disprove an SDS and not prove it. Even when they conform to the expectation from the SDS it is not sufficiently exclusive to do more than support the hypothesis. Hence the null hypothesis is favoured to giving probability figures for the SDS prediction. The tyranny of the null hypothesis, however, limits scientific investigation to confirmatory testing. This not likely to advance knowledge much but gives some degree of confidence for what is called evidence based theories. It is important to realise that these testing methods are useful to support or repudiate theories but that they are not how we actually think. Nor do we think in scientific deductive systems, we think in models. This has great advantages but as Braithwaite pointed out it has disadvantages. He gives us a health warning about using models. If a model is used it brings with it characteristics that are not only extensions of the logical statement it expresses but also some properties of the chosen model. These, as he says, give rise to statements such as "it is true by definition", where in fact the logic of the model has been substituted for the logic of the SDS. Braithwaite gives the example of hydrogen atoms, which behave in certain respects like mini-solar systems. It is useful therefore to think of them as if they were like that model, as long as one keeps in mind that they are not in fact, and whatever they are like is quite different. He also points out that often adherence to existing models survives refutation from further information by further elaboration of the model. Ptolemy's flat earth, geocentric model of the universe survived for a long time despite the fact that the position of the planets contradicted it, because he produced more and more elaborate mathematical explanations that justified the original model.

Braithwaite's ideas were an important source for Bion's meta-psychological thinking. In fact, ingeniously, Bion reversed the Braithwaite scheme, which moves from scientific deductive system through models to particular instances. In his grid he reversed the order of this, ascending from the specific instance through a model (phantasy) to an SDS. In Bion's version primitive experience ascends through phantasy and dream to conceptions (models), ultimately towards an as yet unrealised SDS.

So it seems we bring to the psychoanalytic table our theories in the form of models, where they can be mistaken for descriptions of actual events or abstract, logical statements. In fact they are neither of these; they are the products of human imagination that organises experience into a shape that already exists in the mind.

Models in clinical practice

A meeting ground for scientific, objective models with personal, subjective models is the psychoanalytic consulting room. And I would like to illustrate that from an actual case. It exemplifies how one might encounter a familiar clinical model in working with a patient. The case was one I supervised of a man, Peter, with a severe stammer that had been unsuccessfully treated by a variety of psychiatric methods and speech therapy, and so he had won his way to psychoanalytic psychotherapy in the NHS. He did not work; he was married but did not have sex, and he remained asocial most of the time. He avoided talking to his mother on the phone and wrote typed letters to her. The model which emerged in my mind with this case and discussed with his psychotherapist was that of Herbert Rosenfeld's narcissistic organisation. Eventually to our astonished satisfaction it was described, unprompted, in vivid detail by the patient. In this model the individual is forbidden to become deeply attached to, or communicate freely with any external object by an internal figure or gang that metes out punishment and offers solipsistic solace.

Peter stammered his way through his sessions and in an undeclared way developed a strong positive transference to his woman analyst. The countertransference also was positive but included disturbing, unexpected images of unspoken violence and fears of suicide. In our supervisions we elaborated a model of the patient trying to make contact and being attacked from within by a narcissistic organisation that mutilated his speech. The analyst had little opportunity to say much to Peter who despite his stammer filled the sessions with his talk. As time passed he became more confiding and let her know the full extent of his secrecy and how much he had never divulged some things to anyone including her. It was, he said now, "one chance in a lifetime"; he had never, ever, let anyone know what was in his mind. His mother used to ask him what he was thinking but, he said, "I would rather cut my hands off than let her know." As we were to discover, being touched had to be avoided both physically and metaphorically.

His secrets emerged and we learnt that he talked fluently and without a stammer to himself when he was alone and that he never stammered talking to children or animals. From the age of fourteen he told her there had been a voice in his head that ordered him not to speak and not to get close to anyone. This "other Peter" as he now called it was punishing him after his sessions, particularly when they had been pleasurable. The analysis went through a difficult period for the analyst, as Peter was tempted to harm himself at times by cutting and contemplated suicide. The willingness of his analyst to know all this while remaining attentive and available eased the analysis into less troubled waters.

I cannot do justice briefly to this case in all its complexity; I only want to illustrate the usefulness of the Rosenfeld model in understanding the patient. But before leaving it I would like to illustrate the analogical nature of models in speech and action. Peter always arrived two minutes before his session and was admitted by the receptionist into the waiting room from where the analyst collected him. On one day the analyst arrived a little late and was on the doorstep at the same time as Peter. She therefore opened the door and as she thought led him into the clinic. When she hung up her coat and went to collect him from the waiting room, he was not there. Alarmed, she looked out of the window to see him driving his car out of the car park; she was naturally puzzled and dismayed. A few moments later the receptionist announced her patient was waiting for her. It seems he had driven out, waited a moment before returning and starting again, thus arriving in the clinic in the usual way, being let in by the receptionist. His initial rationalisation was that he had to re-park his car as it had to be a certain minimum distance from any other to avoid touching. Later he acknowledged that being within touching distance of his analyst had unnerved him. His stammer, always of a hesitant repetitive type, had now been reproduced in action, and demonstrated how it regulated proximity and immediacy in an impulsive man afraid of defying his other self by making passionate contact. Some little time after I had written this account, Peter stopped his stammer in his sessions but you will not be surprised to hear that this was followed by a temporary negative therapeutic reaction.

In this example the clinical material coincided with a theoretical model I learnt from Herbert Rosenfeld. Earlier in this chapter I referred to theories, including psychoanalytic theories being couched in the form of models. This has the advantage of allowing further thinking but the disadvantage is that they become the intellectual home for the thinker, and it is not easy to leave a home one is attached to. In both personal and theoretical situations it means leaving a world shaped by a redundant model for a world with an indefinite shape. In an earlier paper I have called this PS(n + 1), a post-depressive position (Britton, 1998).

CHAPTER SEVEN

Myths as models

The first example of the use of a Greek myth as a psychoanalytic model is the Oedipus complex. But it is clear that the model was initially a clinical one and only acquired its mythic dimension later when Freud, on the basis of his self-analysis, turned to Sophocles for support. The first written evidence we have for the idea of the complex is in May 1897 in a letter to his friend Wilhelm Fliess. Freud wrote that he now thought an integral constituent of neuroses was hostile impulse against parents: "This death wish is directed in sons against their father and in daughters against their mother." He wrote a succinct further note: "A maidservant makes a transference from this by wishing her mistress to die so he can marry her (cf. Lisl's dream about Martha and me)" (1897, p. 255). Lisl reported her dream presumably because Freud was recruiting the whole household as dreamers to furnish his emerging work on *The Interpretation of Dreams*. Here is a new clinical model complete with the notion of transformation, from father to professor and from her mother to his wife.

This central model and intense mode of understanding has stayed with psychoanalysis ever since. A little later in the same year it was to acquire the name of Oedipus complex and by being linked to a Greek myth gained a sense of universality. It took its new name from

Sophocles's play *Oedipus Rex* which is based on the myth involving Laius, king of Thebes, his wife Jocasta, their son Oedipus, and the Delphic oracle. Freud described in a letter to Fliess five months after his description of Lisl's dream his discovery of a similar configuration in himself in the course of his own self-analysis. This persuaded him that such wishes might be ubiquitous. And he conjured up for the Greek drama of *Oedipus Rex* an imaginary *universal* audience in which "Each member was once, in germ and in phantasy, just such an Oedipus." Freud refers to the horror generated in the audience by the "dream fulfilment here transplanted into reality" (ibid., p. 265): the horror, that is, of Oedipus killing his father and marrying his mother. It is now a *universal* audience presumed to be possessed of an "Oedipus complex". Freud referred to Oedipus in Sophocles's play in this letter to Fliess in October 1897 and he expanded on the model and on Sophocles's play in *The Interpretation of Dreams* in 1900. There he is explicit that the appeal of the old tragedy is that it tells a universal truth of unconscious wishes. "It is the fate of all of us, perhaps, to direct our first sexual impulses towards our mother and our first hatred and our first murderous wish against our father" (1900a, p. 262). The complex had now become male centred even though most of its early clinical examples were women who entertained the phantasy dreamt by Lisl. It is obvious that Freud identified with Oedipus as did William Wordsworth; both as young men had phantasies of displacing their father and in old age physically depended on their daughters. Freud described Anna as his Antigone.

What attracted my attention to the myth once more was not the Sophocles story but a number of male patients who were haunted by the phantasy that some newcomer would displace them and that they would be discarded. One such had insisted on his wife having an abortion when she became pregnant for the first time. This put me in mind of Laius, Oedipus's father, who was forewarned by the oracle that his child would kill him and take his place.

Sophocles's play *Oedipus Rex* begins at the climactic ending of the story with Oedipus determinedly seeking the cause of a pestilence in Thebes. The chorus and audience witness him finding out that *he* is the pestilence because he has murdered his father and married his mother; as the Delphic oracle said he would. In following the play we need to keep in mind that the original audience knew the myth which included events that preceded the action of the play including the prehistory of the characters. I want to use a different part of the myth to provide another model. In this King Laius is the central character. He has been told by the Delphic oracle that if he has a child he will be deposed and eliminated. The clinical complex I am referring to is one where a man, once he is in a sexual relationship, believes he is bound to be deposed by a figure yet to emerge. This figure inhabits the man's mind leading him to fear it will be realised by the arrival of a stranger who as yet is unknown. I thought of it as an "invisible twin", the twin of the self that remained unborn. In the case of Laius an inner voice, represented in the myth as an oracle, tells him it will be a child born to him and Jocasta. His solution is similar to that of King Herod who, faced with a prediction that a newborn baby will be king of the Jews, had all the newborn babies killed.

The advantage of taking well-established myths as mental models is that further enquiry into them is often helpful in producing a profitable line of enquiry in the clinical cases. So I will give some background to the story of Laius, Jocasta, and Oedipus.

Laius was the son of Labdacus who was king of Thebes. Labdacus made the annual Dionysian rituals illegal. These were celebratory events devoted to the worship of Dionysius (Bacchus), god of drink, drugs, and sex. In modern street language, rock and roll. These events had a reputation for sending women into states of sexual excitation, which made them mad, and dangerous. The Maenads, the enraptured female followers of Dionysius, were so infuriated by the cancellation of their celebrations they assassinated Labdacus (Graves, 1992).

The fear of women given to spontaneous, unsolicited sexual arousal seems to be disturbing to many men. In the myth the fear of female sexuality leads Labdacus, Laius's father, to make the Dionysian rites illegal, a very drastic step. It would be, in the present day, like the mayor of Cologne making the annual carnival permanently illegal, or his counterpart in New Orleans forbidding Mardi Gras. In the myth, female sexuality, personified as the Maenads, makes women powerful and potentially murderous. In the modern German five-day feast of *Karneval*, or *Fasching*, the Friday is traditionally reserved for women to choose their sexual partners. The event climaxes on the following Tuesday (Shrove Tuesday in England) before giving way to Ash Wednesday, a day of repentance and confession and the first day of Lenten abstinence. A period of cleansing by abstinence is practised by all three of the great Abrahamic religions, Judaism, Christianity, and Islam, which have their genesis in symbolic sacrifice to a single god, whereas in the Greek mythology it is the gods representing conflicting tendencies who compete for devotion.

Laius inherited his father's kingdom but he was only five when his father died. Laius was eventually established as king of Thebes and then married Jocasta; they did not manage to have children so he consulted the Delphic oracle. The oracle, as was the way of oracles, rather like psychoanalysts, did not answer questions but made statements that were famous for being ambiguous. This one, however, was not ambiguous: the oracle said do not have children as your child will kill you and take your place. Laius therefore ceased to have sexual relations with Jocasta who was furious. So on one occasion, with the aid of wine, she seduced him, thus conceiving Oedipus (ibid.). Many years later, "at a place where three roads meet", Laius meets an intrusive stranger who unknowingly fulfils the prophecy (Sophocles, p. 46). What better diagrammatic representation could there be than "where three roads meet", for the vagina where the two legs are joined to the female torso. It is also the conjunction of two prophecies of the Delphic oracle, one given to Laius as the husband of Jocasta and the other to Oedipus as her son, and it fulfils both. The vagina is the meeting place of entry and exit, of conception and birth. In the myth Laius is leaving Thebes and Jocasta for Delphi whilst Oedipus is journeying from Delphi towards Thebes where he will ultimately enter Jocasta. Their places are already reversed symbolically; Laius is born again en route to consult the oracle whilst Oedipus is about to impregnate his mother.

This seems to me to complete a circle begun with Laius's father Labdacus, who made Dionysian female sexuality illegal and was killed as a result by the Maenads. His son, Laius, following the advice of the oracle stops having sex with his wife, Jocasta; she is furious and with the aid of wine seduces him thus giving birth to Oedipus who is fated to kill him. Labdacus the father is killed for stopping female sexuality and his son Laius is killed as a consequence of succumbing to it. For men it seems, in Greek myths as in life, sexuality is felt to be dangerous when appropriated by and emanating from women. The mythic stories of Dionysian celebrations are full of accounts of women driven mad by sex and alcohol, seen as sexually abandoned, unrestrained, and dangerous.

A dream of a patient illustrates this: he is in bed with two women on either side of him. Both women are his wife, but are very different. The one on his right is sexually very provocative and insistent sexually;

the one on his left is as his wife usually is, responsive but not given to initiating sexuality. He is very disturbed by the sexy version of his wife and repelled by her. He calls her an abandoned woman and pushes her away. When I commented that he was alarmed by the uninvited, spontaneous sexuality of women he recalled an affair in his youth when he was horrified by the sexual avidity and promiscuity of a girl friend.

The double meaning of the word "abandoned" seems significant. It is used to describe a woman who gives herself over to sexuality and as abandonment to being left by someone. A child might well feel abandoned by a mother who has abandoned herself to her sexual partner. So we return to the familiar model of the primal scene, which Klein described as the Oedipal situation.

To this, in order to complete the model, we need to add a new arrival, a stranger. In the myth this stranger, who kills Laius and takes his wife, turns out to be a child from her womb, Oedipus, the unintended and unexpected, the child who should have remained unborn. This new arrival is the consequence of Jocasta's sexual desire defying the warnings of the oracle. In Sophocles's play Jocasta is portrayed as an opponent of oracles and a sceptic of their veracity. She is triumphant when she thinks, wrongly as it turns out, that there is news that contradicts the oracular prediction. Somewhat surprisingly she says to Oedipus:

> Chance rules our lives, and the future is all unknown.
> Best live as best we may, from day to day.
> Nor need this mother-marrying frighten you;
> Many a man has dreamt as much. (Sophocles, p. 52)

There is a sense that as a woman she is tired of this masculine preoccupation with oracular verbal pronouncements (indirectly from Apollo), rather like Job's wife's irritation with Job because he continues to be preoccupied by his relationship with a God who inflicts misfortunes on him.

My exploration of the myth has led me to think that a masculine fear of erotic desire and sexual pleasure in women is basic to what we might call a Laius complex. The treatment of women in a number of cultures worldwide would seem consonant with this, perhaps the most extreme example being female circumcision, which seems so resistant to Western liberal culture. Religious rules and rituals that seek to limit and gain control over female sexuality are recurrent in all three of the great Abrahamic religions, Judaism, Christianity, and Islam all of which have extremist sects where female sexuality is severely curtailed.

In order to take this model further I would like to briefly discuss two patients.

The first is a professor of history in late middle age who had come to a second analysis because he thought there was something unresolved in the first. He was now happy in a second marriage and successful in his work but he could not understand why he still felt uncertain of his position and place in both situations. His father had died young when he was in his late teens and he had an older brother but no younger siblings. His older brother it was thought would take over from the father in the care of the home but he did not do so and left for university. His mother turned to him to complete the various domestic projects of his father's that were unfinished. He understood from his first analysis how he had always played second fiddle to his brother and to men in his working life whose position resembled that of an older brother. Once again in his new analysis he met this pattern in the transference and in addition the transference anxiety that his new analyst, a man, would like his father die prematurely leaving him overwhelmed by various new responsibilities arising from his second marriage. What new psychic developments emerged, however, concerned his unjustified reactions to his wife's enthusiastic professional activities. She was a poet and like most poets belonged to a small workshop of colleagues. He admired her work and loved poetry but now felt he was not entitled to enjoy poetry any more as he was not a practitioner. This was analysed in terms of his recollection of his parents' sexual relationship which, when he encountered it, made him feel that the sexual feelings he actually had as a child were inappropriate and unnatural. As a consequence he did not masturbate until quite late in adolescence. This analytic understanding seemed to relieve him of his inhibition of poetically induced emotional reaction. But as time went on and his attachment both to his analyst and to his wife deepened the problem of his reaction to his wife's poetic enthusiasm intensified. It crystallised one weekend.

He returned for the first session of the week commenting that he once again found he approached his Monday session with a feeling of dread; this had been a new development of some few weeks. He went on to comment that the weekend had been a very happy one until there was a crash in his feelings on the Saturday night and since then he had been feeling desperate. He reported that his wife had been to her poetry workshop and he had been happily busy with his notes. She returned, he said, with her eyes bright and excited: they had done such good work on a presented poem. He was very conscious of the fact that one newish member of this group was a young, foreign poet whose work she admired. The patient said nothing to his wife but felt desolate. He became detached and morose without any explanation. I commented that her pleasure and excitement disturbed him though she shared her enthusiasm with him. "Yes," he responded, "I felt I had lost her and was now a complete outsider." We were able to link this with another new development that had been leading to these feelings of dread on Mondays. He now had the idea, one year after beginning his analysis, that I was excited at the prospect of new analytic work and was probably going to take a new patient. The other link was in his history: what had been emerging was that after his father's death his mother had become sexually active and that he knew it because he had witnessed it in part at least. He had "forgotten" this until recently or denied knowing it most of his life. It emerged in analysis as a result of some dream interpretation.

The arrival of a new man is evident in the patient's intrinsic narrative, or model, but what I particularly wish to emphasise is the reaction to his wife's literary excitement. This is conflated in his mind with sexual excitement and it turns her into an unpredictable woman in the grip of aberrant, sexual feelings, quite at odds with his usual picture of her as reassuring, reliable, devoted, and sensible. She is in his imagination a woman losing her common sense by sexual excitement and losing her judgement in relation to a newcomer. It is also like a mother being transformed into one of a pair of lovers in the primal scene.

This is an example of a clinical model looking for a myth to exemplify it: the role of the myth is to suggest it has universality. I was struck by a particular clinical pattern. It was one where an involvement in a serious love relationship in a man gave rise to a fearful expectation of his being deposed by a yet unknown, unseen stranger. It was as if there was an invisible twin, an eternally potential presence, who had not yet materialised but might at any moment. I found other clinical examples in which this complex of fearful expectation was initiated not by failure but by sexual success. In all these cases I surmised that though they had been welcomed as infants and young children, for one reason or another they were not the idealised infant who existed in the mother's mind during her pregnancy. Put another way they were not after all the "Messiah". I have suggested elsewhere, that the "ego ideal", the Messiah, is based on the anticipated prenatal infant in the parental mind. Here I am suggesting that if the discrepancy between the prospective ideal infant of the maternal mind and the mother's reaction to the actual infant is in some way communicated to the child it can give rise to the phantasy that there was an invisible twin who might yet emerge.

There is huge hinterland to the myth of Laius, Oedipus, and Jocasta. When I researched it I realised how extraordinarily the network of Greek myths proliferate and connect, like free associations. They are intertwined but not integrated into one narrative, unlike the Hebrew bible story. In that respect they are like the psychoanalytic models that have accumulated since Freud opened the book with the Oedipus complex: intertwined but not really integrated. Two themes impressed me as illuminating the clinical material I was addressing. One, fear of displacement by the newcomer which, I postulate, is of the as yet unborn sibling. Another is the male fear of female sexuality, or to be more precise female desire and pleasure.

Dionysius the god of fertility, sexual pleasure, and wine had fervent female followers. Dionysius was called the twice born, once out of his earthly mother Semele and once out of Zeus his father. He was therefore seen as exemplifying both patrilineal and matrilineal descent. Jealous Hera, Zeus's wife, had tricked Semele into insisting to her lover Zeus that he disclose his real identity by refusing him access to her bed. Zeus retaliated by striking her dead with lightning. She was six months pregnant and her unborn son Dionysius was plucked from her womb and saved by being placed in Zeus's thigh, emerging three months later. Mythology has him born as a serpent in winter, becoming a lion in the spring and a bull in midsummer. There was also a celebration called the Festival of the Wild Women in which the bull, representing Dionysius, was killed, cut into nine pieces, one of which was burnt as an offering to Semele his mother, and the other eight eaten raw by the priestesses.

It seems from this that there were two particular male fears of female sexual reproduction. One, the latent fear of the newcomer, which I have called the invisible twin; the other is fear of sexually aroused women becoming vengeful, mad, and dangerous. This latter idea helped me to understand a case brought to me for consultation by an analytic colleague who thought there was a serious crisis in the analysis. She was an experienced and very able woman analyst who became alarmed by the increasingly disturbed mental state of her male patient; her fears were compounded when he said things were going from bad to worse and that the analysis had to stop.

He was a middle-aged man who came to the analysis as a consequence of his depression following an unfortunate incident in his professional life. He was an academic who supervised postgraduate students, one of whom developed a crush on him and became in effect a female stalker, ringing him at home, following him to restaurants, and soliciting his attention out of hours. He felt obliged to collude with her to the extent of socialising in this way outside their tutorial hours. Meanwhile he took advice from a senior colleague who urged him to prevent any contact outside her tutorials. He failed to do this and continued colluding with her flirtatious activities. His exasperated senior colleague insisted that he stop the woman's tutorials altogether, which he reluctantly did, with difficulty and grave misgivings; she committed suicide shortly afterwards. The man was distraught and sought psychiatric help and from there found his way into analysis with my colleague. This relieved him considerably initially and he settled into the analysis and was able to resume work. The consultation I had with my colleague was two years later because she thought there was now a crisis. She had realised that he had developed an erotic transference, which she did not directly confront but indirectly referred to. Explicit sexual dream material involving her was brought to the sessions. He became increasingly agitated in the analysis saying that something was not working, something was going wrong and he must stop the analysis. The analyst who was also a psychiatrist was very concerned about his mental state and feared what would happen if he stopped, conscious of the history of suicide.

I asked in the consultation about the transference and her countertransference. Basing my thoughts on my conviction that a sustained, intense, conscious erotic transference is always believed by a patient to be reciprocated by the analyst, I asked how he had been treating her. She told me that he seemed concerned about her health recently and had commented on her voice being different; she felt he was observing her closely and preoccupied about her. I suggested to her that her patient believed his erotic feelings were reciprocated and he thought that she was aroused sexually in the analytic sessions, which he regarded as dangerous for her. She, I suggested, should say that he was worried about her because he thought she was sexually stimulated by what he was bringing to her and that it was driving her mad. This she was able to say and was surprised by his ready acceptance of this interpretation, confirming that he did think he had this effect on her. This relieved the situation for both of them. It seems that he, like Labdacus and other men in the Greek myths, thought that sexual desire and physical arousal drove women mad.

I think it is true to say that I turned to studying the Oedipus myth because I had already a clinical model in mind that seemed exemplified by the story of Laius. But the further reaches of the mythic story led me to Labdacus and the Maenads and that provided me with a model of male phantasy about the effect of sexual excitation in women. This in turn provided a potential clinical model: the to and fro of this kind of model-making has exemplified psychoanalysis from its outset in 1897.

CHAPTER EIGHT

The triangular model

I first wrote about what I called triangular space and the third position in a paper given in 1987 at a conference at University College London on "The Oedipus Complex Today". I wrote:

> The acknowledgement by the child of the parents' relationship with each other unites his psychic world, limiting it to one world shared with his two parents in which different object relationships can exist. The closure of the Oedipal triangle by the recognition of the link joining the parents provides a limiting boundary for the internal world. It creates what I call a "triangular space", i.e., a space bounded by the three persons of the Oedipal situation and all their potential relationships. It includes, therefore, the possibility of being a participant in a relationship and observed by a third person as well as being an observer of a relationship between two people ...
>
> If the link between the parents perceived in love and hate can be tolerated in the child's mind, it provides him with a prototype for an object relationship of a third kind in which he is a witness and not a participant. A third position then comes into existence from which object relationships can be observed. Given this, we

> can also envisage being observed. This provides us with a capacity
> for seeing ourselves in interaction with others and for entertain-
> ing another point of view whilst retaining our own, for reflecting
> on ourselves whilst being ourselves. This is a capacity we hope
> to find in ourselves and in our patients in analysis. (Britton, 1989,
> pp. 86–87)

The theorising in the paper came from experiences with borderline
patients with whom for long periods of time this capacity was missing.
It gradually became evident to me in these cases that what was missing
was the "third position" described above. I came to realise that efforts
of mine to consult my analytic self were detected by such patients and
experienced as a form of internal intercourse of mine, which corresponded to parental intercourse. This they felt threatened their existence. The only way I found of finding a place to think that was helpful
and not disruptive was to allow the evolution within myself of my own
experience and *to articulate this to myself*, while communicating with the
patients my *understanding of their point of view*. The possibility of my
communicating with a third object was unthinkable and so the third
position I refer to was untenable. The third object in such cases could be
my theories, links with colleagues, or the residue of previous analytic
experience.

As a consequence it seemed impossible to disentangle oneself
sufficiently from the to-and-fro of the interaction to know what was
going on. Any move towards objectivity could not be tolerated. Analyst
and patient were to move along a single line and meet at a single
point. There was to be no lateral movement. A sense of space could be
achieved only by increasing the distance between us, a process such
patients find impossible to bear unless they initiate it. In such situations
what I felt I needed desperately was a place in my mind that I could
step into sideways, from which I could look at things. If I tried to force
myself into such a position by asserting a description of the patient in
my own terms, violence would follow, always psychically, sometimes
also physically.

I arrived at the model of triangular space and the third position
from particular clinical experiences. My theorising was based essentially on Melanie Klein's model of the early Oedipal situation (1928)
and Bion's model of the container/contained (1959, 1962a, 1962b). He
had described that for some individuals the consequences of a failure of maternal containment was the development of a destructive

superego that prevents them from learning or pursuing profitable relations with any object. He made it clear that the inability of the mother to take in her child's projections is experienced *by the child* as a destructive attack *by her* on his link and communication *with her* as his good object.

I suggested that belief in a good maternal object in these circumstances can only be regained by splitting off her perceived hostility to linkage and attributing it to a third, a hostile force, such a force as that represented in various religions of the ancient world as "chaos monsters": in ancient Egypt it was Apophis. He "... was an embodiment of primordial chaos. He had no sense-organs, he could neither hear nor see, he could only scream. And he operated always in darkness" (Cohn, 1993, p. 21). He continually threatened *ma'at*, the female personification of order in the world, as she travelled through the hours of darkness. Mother as the source of goodness, like ma'at, is now precarious and depends on the child restricting his thoughts of her to the light of day and banishing his imagination of her night-time activities.

Enlargement of knowledge of her, as a consequence of cognitive development and his curiosity, are felt to menace this crucial relationship. Curiosity discloses the existence of the Oedipal situation. The hostile force, the chaos monster that was thought to attack his link with his mother, is now equated with the Oedipal father, and her link to him is felt to destroy her as a source of goodness and order. I am suggesting that the problem has its origins in the relationship to the primary maternal object when there is failure to establish an unequivocally good experience of the infant–mother interaction to contrast with the bad experience of being deprived of it. Instead of the natural primary split between experientially good and bad objects in the paranoid schizoid position there is confusion. To arrest the confusion an arbitrary split in mental life is imposed to enshrine the notion of good and to locate and segregate the bad. The essential structure of the Oedipal situation lends itself to splitting of this kind. This can give rise to the misleading appearance of being a classical, positive Oedipus complex based on rivalry with mother for the love of father. The transference tells another tale. The familiar split configuration of the positive Oedipal configuration which is usually used to separate love and hate, in these cases is used to provide a structure to segregate desire for subjective understanding and love from the wish for objective knowledge and a shared intellectual identity. I have come to regard these as being the characteristics of *the narcissistic and borderline disorders.*

Narcissistic disorders

Henri Rey described these syndromes as, "… a certain kind of personality disorder which defied classification into the two great divisions of neurosis and psychosis. We now know them as borderline, narcissistic, or schizoid personality organization" (1979, p. 203). What sufferers of these various syndromes have in common is that they cannot, at least initially, function in analysis in an ordinary way because they cannot form an ordinary transference relationship. Some remain aloof and detached; others are adherent, clamorous, and concrete in their transference attachment. But in neither of these is the analyst experienced *as both significant and separate*.

Rosenfeld described some patients as thick-skinned narcissistic patients in contrast to thin-skinned narcissistic patients. He wrote:

> There are those whose narcissistic structure provides them with such a "thick skin" that they have become insensitive to deeper feelings, to avoid impasse these patients have to be treated in analysis very firmly … When interpretations at last manage to touch them they are relieved, even if it is painful to them … By contrast … the thin skinned patients are hypersensitive and easily hurt in everyday life and analysis. Moreover, when the sensitive narcissistic patient is treated in analysis as if he is the thick skinned patient he will be severely traumatized. (1987, p. 274)

I suggest that these two states are the result of two different relationships of the *subjective self* to the *third object* in the internal Oedipus triangle. In both states the third object is alien to the subjective, sensitive self. In the hyper-subjective case the self seeks to avoid the third object and clings to subjectivity. The hyper-objective patient identifies with the third object and adopts a mode of objectivity by renouncing subjectivity (Britton, 1998).

What is quickly revealed in both cases is that analysis is a major problem for such patients or for their analyst. Being in analysis is a problem; being in the same room; being in the same mental space. Instead of there being two connected, independent minds there are either two separate people unable to connect or two people with only one mind. These two situations could not be more different from each other in analysis. What they have in common is their inability to function in an ordinary way and their terror of the integration of separate minds.

In the one group *the other* is treated as of no significance, in the second group the patient cannot commune without making *the significant other* an extension of himself or herself. In the first situation the analyst cannot find a place within the psychic reality of the patient, in the second the analyst cannot find a place outside it. The first is hyper-objective with narcissistic detachment and the second is hyper-subjective with narcissistic adherence.

Here are examples of the two models, first that of hyper-objectivity and narcissistic detachment, the thick-skinned patients. The patient was a successful writer seeking analysis after a period of marital therapy at the suggestion of the therapist and with the prompting of his wife. He told me this and added with disarming frankness that his problem was intimacy. "I am no good at intimate relations, my wife tells me, and I am sure she is right." He also let me know in the consultation that he had suffered from depression of a kind in which he would wake sick with a sense of terror, and despair about life in general and his own uselessness. When he was young and still religious he believed that he was damned and beyond redemption and that the usual religious remedies, of confession, contrition, etc. would not work for him. When I suggested that he might feel the same about analysis he quickly agreed that he could not imagine it helping or changing him in the slightest, "[B]ut I have to try it if you are willing to have a go," he said.

The problem of shared analytic space quickly asserted itself when he arrived for the first session. We agreed a time and he accepted the analytic conventions as he saw them of lying on a couch for fifty minutes. But he conveyed that he could have done so equally willingly if I suggested standing on his head for fifty minutes. "Enduring things", I suggested, "is something you know you can do without them having any effect on you." He agreed with this and offered me several convincing examples from his childhood of his fortitude protecting him from being changed by the regimes inflicted on him. Once we got underway the problem was mine. Though I could without too much difficulty understand him, I could not find a means of sharing his mental space, of getting into contact with him. I was the "outsider" in this analysis. The patient would claim that he was not really involved in the analysis and sympathised with me for having to endure such an unappreciative patient when presumably I would like to be thought important and my ideas appreciated. My needs therefore were worth his consideration but he could not do anything about it. Pity was what he offered me, as a decrepit old man, that he once described as the West Hampstead worm.

I was not empty–minded, however, outside the realm of his attention. He had a gift for communicating to me what difficulties faced him and what anxieties troubled him so that I was vividly aware of his very real suffering and predicament. If I drew attention to these he politely scoffed at me for taking them seriously. He would then leave the session on an upbeat note of "Begone, dull cares" and with a wave say "See you tomorrow." I was left in other words "holding the baby". This applied also to his memories, to his recollections of cruel experience, to his revelations of painful humiliations and considerable deprivation.

He treated my opinion that he had suffered an unhappy childhood as eccentric. If I then reminded him of the recollections he had disclosed in the previous session he would quickly say he had a terrible memory and forgot everything from one day to another. So I was the only one who now knew of the existence of the suffering child. My patient had gone missing. When I suggested to him that he emptied his experiential self into me and that when he left the session he left two of us behind and went out empty, he responded by describing to me a story he had worked on. It had a title but he said, "It should have been entitled '*The story of a missing person*'." In this story someone was exploring a residence and could not establish whether anyone lived there or not. They could see the outline of the missing person's life, like an impression on the bed, and the details of somebody's day from traces left behind, but there was no presence. The essence of the story was that of absence, as emptiness with the shape of a missing person.

In analysis as in marriage absence appears to solve the problem of presence. However, it requires a place from which to be absent. In order to be an absentee husband you need a wife, or to be an absentee patient you need an analyst, or to be a runaway you need a home to run away from. To have a missed session you need to have a session arranged.

Largely through the use of my own countertransference as a source of information about my missing patient we were able to get some idea of the problems that led to his "psychic retreat" to the periphery of his own life. I found that while retaining my usual analytic position of receptivity and inquiry I could not achieve my customary sense of significance or presence. I was tempted to insert myself into my patient's field by assuming a role already assigned to me often as a coach or a friendly critic. The price to be paid in the countertransference for remaining in my own psychic sphere, for being myself was a sense of insignificance and loneliness. This it was not difficult to see was my patient's experience in the past and in his present working life where he felt he was always on the rim of the world. Here on the edge he could define himself as the outsider, as the man who would not fit in. The cost of this identity was exclusion. The passport to inclusion was to be defined by the other's presuppositions and preconceptions; the price for entry into the mind of the other was to allow oneself to be misperceived. The sacrifice to be made to secure a place indoors was to be caged within the limiting framework of the other's comprehension of the world.

As a child he found a hideaway where he could be unknown to the family. His dreams made clear how significant this secret space was and how it was the forerunner of other private spaces culminating in the creation of the study where he worked. Here he created in his own writing his own versions of himself and placed these replicas in a variety of contexts of his own choosing that accurately mirrored his internal world. And a bleak and lonely place it usually was for these creations. I was to get inside knowledge of this bleak terrain because it was where he placed me in the analysis. We met there eventually in a shared moorland-like mental landscape that felt reminiscent to me of that in which Wordsworth met the leech-gatherer when driven to despair by Coleridge's "Ode to Dejection". My impression was that he benefited from his analysis; certainly he prospered. I would like to think that our encounter might have had a similar therapeutic effect on him as that which Wordsworth ascribed to the leech-gatherer whose fortitude regenerated hope in him, "… to find/ In that decrepit Man so firm a mind" (Selincourt & Darbishire, 1940, p. 156).

The second group I see as characterised by their hyper-subjectivity and narcissistic adherence. What clinically characterises this group of cases is their *difficulty*. They find life with others difficult; they find tolerating themselves difficult; they find being in analysis difficult, and in a characteristic way, their analysts find working with them difficult. When analysts bring such cases for consultation they almost always begin by saying, "I want to talk to you about my difficult patient," or "I seem to have particular difficulty with this case." It is often accompanied by a sense of shame in the analysts who feel either that they have let the patient down or that they have become involved in a collusive analysis in a way they are reluctant to acknowledge to colleagues.

Of course, many patients pose considerable technical and counter-transference problems but the characteristic problem that leads analysts to use the word *difficult* with such emphasis is of a particular kind. It is the way that the analytic method itself is felt by the patient to be a threat, its structure, its method, and its boundaries. The corollary of that in the analyst is a feeling that she (let us say) can never properly establish an analytic setting. Some analysts have used this impasse to promote as a superior analytic method an alternative strategy that in reality was dictated by the patient as a necessary condition. This I think corresponds with a belief of the patient, secret or not, that his atypical method of growing up was a more authentic way and that ordinary children who become more tractable analytic patients are either victims of oppression or are collaborators.

While the analyst is working empathetically with her patient and validating his subjective experience in a way he finds helpful, the analyst finds herself to be like a mother who does not really exist in her own right. The patient feels very reliant on this function and on the analyst as this receptive figure, but the analyst fears she has lost her analytic identity. If, however, the analyst asserts herself and produces objectively based interpretations she will feel persecuted and then either submit in a masochistic way, or explode. She will, one way or another, eliminate what he says or eradicate the elements in it of difference. She may feel the need to remove her mind from his presence by psychic withdrawal, and some patients find it necessary to remove their bodies in order to remove their minds and so break off analysis. These patients are inclined to leave some analysts or stay in an impasse with others. The risks are of analytic abortion or interminable analysis. Subjective and objective realities are believed to be more than simply incompatible, to be, in fact, mutually destructive.

Objectivity appears to be associated with gaze. There is a fear of being seen just as there is a fear of being described. A child with such problems in psychoanalytic psychotherapy serves well as an example because of the directness of the exchange with the psychotherapist. In a case I supervised a seven-year-old girl was clearly very persecuted simply by being in the therapist's room and screamed whenever he tried to speak. Eventually, with his help, she managed to make it clear to him that if she blindfolded and gagged him so that he could not see, or speak, but only listen, then she would talk to him. When he was able to say to her that she believed his words would spoil and mess up her thoughts she burst out," They will, they will! So shut up!"

Such situations in their adult versions can evoke existential anxieties in an analyst because his empathic identification with the patient seems incompatible with his objective clinical view of the situation and his ideas of what is necessary. Therefore he feels cut off from the theories that link him to his colleagues and that give him his professional identity. It also manifests itself as a difficulty for the analyst in using his general experience or his general ideas, as this appears to intrude on the singularity of the encounter with his patient and the particularity of his patient's psychology. Particularity seems to be at war with generality in much the same way as subjectivity is with objectivity. In terms of the figures of the Oedipal triangle, while the analyst is able to follow and enhance the patient's emergent thoughts he is identified as an understanding maternal object. When introducing thoughts of his own derived from his general experience and analytic theories he is identified as a father who is either intruding into the patient's innermost self or pulling the patient out of her subjective psychic context into one of his own.

So we have a defensively organised Oedipal situation with the phantasy of a totally empathic, passively understanding maternal object and an aggressive paternal figure who is objectivity personified seeking to impose meaning. While this defensive organisation of the Oedipal triangle is maintained it guarantees that reintegration will never take place between the understanding object and the misunderstanding object that would result, it is believed, in the annihilation of understanding. In this hyper-subjective mode, the positive transference expresses its energy not by penetration but by extrapolation. Its intensity is expressed by extension. It encompasses the object and invests everything it covers with heightened significance. The physical person of the analyst and by extension the contextual details of the analysis are given great importance, such as the minutiae of sessions, the room and its contents, and so on. Patients may collect and retain remnants of the analysis such as bills, paper tissues, etc. that serve a similar function to religious relics. The negative transference is equated with a penetrating third object, while feeling understood is attributed to the primary object. Both positive and negative transferences are in play: one craved for and sought after, the other dreaded and evaded. The desired transference is skin deep and enveloping. Its epistemological mode is empathy, its physical expression is touch, and its emotional qualities are erotic or aesthetic. What is dreaded most is the conjunction of the encompassing transference with the penetrating transference, that is, of subjectivity with objectivity.

From the transference it seems that the basic fear is of *malignant misunderstanding*. By this I mean an experience of being so *misunderstood* in such a fundamental and powerful way that one's experience of oneself would be eliminated and with it the possibility of the self-establishing meaning would be annihilated. When there is a desire for understanding coupled with a dread of misunderstanding there is an insistent, desperate need for agreement in the analysis and annihilation of disagreement. I have come to believe that there is a general rule arising from anxiety about misunderstanding which applies in all analyses: it is that *the need for agreement is inversely proportional to the expectation of understanding*. When expectation of understanding is high difference of opinion is tolerable, where expectation of understanding is fairly high difference is fairly tolerable, when there is no expectation of understanding the need for agreement is absolute.

Is there something in *the temperament* of some individuals that *predisposes* them to this particular development or response to trauma? Is there anything in the endowment of these individuals that might encourage them to believe that an independently existing object will destructively misunderstand them? Is there *an innate factor* in the infant that increases the risk of a *failure of maternal containment* and if so what might it be? I think there can be an allergy to the products of other minds, analogous with the body's immune system, a kind of *psychic atopia*. The immune system is central to our physiological functioning: our physiological integrity is at stake; we cannot survive without it and yet it is often the source of pathology. Is the same true of our psychic functioning? It certainly appears to be in our social functioning where the annihilation of the perceived alien is commonplace. The *not me* or *not like me* recognition and response might fulfil a similar psychic function as it does in the somatic. And just as the immune system sometimes makes for physiological trouble between mothers and babies, as in the familiar rhesus incompatibility problem, so perhaps might there be troublesome psychic immunity responses. Are there psychic allergies and is there sometimes psychic autoimmunity? In the realm of ideas and understanding we do seem to behave as if we have a psychic immune system. We are fearful for the integrity of our existing belief systems and whenever we encounter foreign psychic material it stimulates a xenocidal impulse. Analysis by producing a shared mental space exposes these difficulties; consequently it provides an opportunity for exploring them.

CHAPTER NINE

Religious fanaticism and ideological genocide

R eligion has become a serious scientific subject in this century because we have realised that when it is taken very seriously it is potentially dangerous. "Generally speaking," said David Hume, the eighteenth-century philosopher, "the errors in religion are dangerous; those in philosophy only ridiculous" (Ayer & O'Grady, 1992, p. 197). Hume was writing at a time now called the Enlightenment when philosophy ceased to be God centred and became man centred. Alexander Pope, the poet, wrote in the same period:

> Know then thyself, presume not God to scan,
> The proper study of mankind is man ...
> (Untermeyer, 1961 p. 260)

Hume like Pope could take his reasoning lightly, as an intellectual pleasure, because there is safety in scepticism. The counter to religion and danger could be scepticism and safety. "Sceptical space is the only hope we have of avoiding endless Creed Wars," (Russell, 1928, p. 13). It is the kind of scepticism that permeates Freud's thinking. Hume's aphorism, "Reason is, and ought to be the slave of the passions, and can never pretend to any other office than to serve and obey them"

(Ayer & O'Grady, 1992, p. 197), is an earlier version of Freud's notion that the reality principle serves the pleasure principle. But the man who can make such a proposition is clearly not the slave of his own passionate beliefs: such sceptics whether they be Spinoza, Hume, or Freud are emancipated from their own beliefs by their capacity to entertain non-destructive doubts. All three of them were able to see man's religious anthropomorphism and his conviction that he lived in a God-created, man-centred universe. The realisation that "God" was man-made in his own image dawned on Spinoza who said if he were a triangle he would think God was triangular.

Hume was the most radical of sceptical philosophers; he claimed that inductive reasoning could not be justified logically or cause and effect established. He was writing in a brief historical period of cool reason after the horrors of the thirty-year religious war in Europe and before the French and American Revolutions and the subsequent Napoleonic wars. No one could say after those revolutions and the violent events that followed them that errors in philosophy are only ridiculous: like those in religion they are potentially dangerous.

It is commonly said by politicians and religious leaders that it is not belief but only violence that is reprehensible. However, it is clear that violence springs from the way the belief systems are held. It is also clear that this has applied to religious and political belief systems of many kinds. The purging of deviance and deviants from a fundamentalist belief system is not confined to supernatural religion. In the twentieth century notable examples are those of the political regimes of Stalin, Hitler, and Pol Pot, in the eighteenth century that of Robespierre. In these instances I would describe them as possessed by an absolutist belief in a political ideology. No country is exempt from the processes that can lead to this phenomenon and no religion appears to be exempt from this form of regression.

My thesis in this chapter is that *it is not what someone believes, it is how they believe it* that determines whether or not destructiveness will be the outcome; it is not what you read but how you read it, whether it is the Hebrew Bible, the Christian Bible, the Koran, or *Das Kapital*. Pol Pot like Stalin based his absolutism on his personal reading of Marx, Hitler on his of Nietzsche, Robespierre on his reading of Rousseau.

For centuries philosophy was the handmaid of religion; since it ceased to be God-centred it has been either the handmaid of science or of politics. Now we are alarmed when we see that political philosophy could once more become the handmaid of religion. There is one theory from our psychoanalytic conceptual store that is both relevant and alarming in this context; that is regression. We in psychoanalysis consider that early and archaic beliefs can continue a subterranean existence, only surfacing in dreams, fictions, and uncanny moments while we are in a state of mental health, but that the "would-be rational ego" can be overwhelmed at other times. Regression is not only a theoretical concept it is in psychoanalytic practice an empirical observation. By analogy can we extend this notion to society and ask, can the belief systems of societies regress?

My title suggests that religion can be fanatical; an alternative word I will use is extreme. We can apply it as in religious extremist or political extremist. In either case it implies that some people have departed from the state of moderate scepticism that has characterised Western society since the seventeenth century. By post-Enlightenment standards the beliefs of ordinary medieval Christians would be seen as fanatical if held by a group, psychotic if held by an individual. Once the Reformation arrived denouncing praying to statues or relics as idolatrous, they largely substituted the word of God in the form of the newly translated Bible. We now would describe the ordinary Protestant beliefs in the Bible in the seventeenth century as fundamentalist. They were believed strongly enough on either side of idolatry or fundamentalism for people holding the wrong one to be burned.

Scepticism is a psychic and cultural development, an achievement, and one not easily won and it seems one rather too easily lost. After a bloody beginning in the sixteenth and seventeenth century the Church of England settled down to become a national church that practised religious nationalism rather than doctrinal Christianity. In the nineteenth century its main preoccupation was personal morality and social stability. By the twentieth century it had become a broad church of diluted convictions, liberal sentiment, democratic values, and aesthetic practice. Such was its containment of contradictory doctrines, in order to be really comfortable in it one needed to be an agnostic. Now the Anglican Church is threatened by a split between its older liberal sceptics whose attachment is to religious sentiment, ethical values, and aesthetic practices, and its very serious-minded, Bible-based doctrinal believers of the evangelical movement. They are the Gnostics, the holders of certainty, the "enthusiasts"; they are not going to leave their beliefs behind in the Sunday church or their metaphysics in the philosopher's study;

they are going to take them into family life and into the street. If they have their way they will also take them into government. They, like their Muslim and Jewish counterparts, would probably be described as fundamentalists who would like a theocracy. State law based on canon law (church law) is the Christian counterpart to Sharia law.

Nowadays the word fundamentalism appears daily in our newspapers and is applied to any religious zealots. But when, in 1988, I gave a paper on "Fundamentalism and Idolatry" it was not so commonplace (Britton, 1993). The term "fundamentalist" was originally derived from a series of tracts called, "The Fundamentals", published in the USA in 1909. These tracts based their authority on the infallibility of the Bible because it was said every word in it was the Word of God. The movement had two particular hated targets, Roman Catholicism and modernism. Both were regarded as idolatrous. Mine was essentially a clinical psychoanalytic paper and I borrowed the religious terms fundamentalism and idolatry in order to apply them to particular phenomena in the analysis of some patients with narcissistic disorders. In these cases the two modes existed as alternatives and were in opposition to each other. Where the analyst's words were *idealised* I called it "word worship", in the other where his physical identity was *idolised* "thing worship", hence fundamentalism and idolatry.

As I related I encountered this split clinically both ways around. To clarify this I will describe briefly an example of each of these kinds of patient. In the first objective understanding was valued and the analyst's words idealised but his physicality was anathema. In the second there was idolisation of the analyst and sublime mutual agreement was only threatened by what he might say.

In the first case words were welcome but awareness of the analyst's physical existence was anathema. The patient, Professor M was a mathematician. Her previous calm reasonableness was now interrupted by anxiety and her usual optimism periodically shattered by episodes of *blackness of vision and boundless terrifying emptiness* in which she could no longer reason but only dread. She referred to these episodes as *the dark night of the soul* and the place she felt she was in as *the void*. She longed to escape from them into sleep or even better into death; she hoped to arrange for a planned death should she ever become physically ill. There was a sense in which she felt trapped in her body.

She quickly made clear that she had throughout life oriented herself by knowing that she hated her mother and loved her father. In particular she was averse to her mother physically and any thought of contact with her made her feel nauseous. She feared chaos if anything to do with her maternal relationship should ever enter into the world of order provided by her own systematic thinking which she identified with her father who had been a mathematician. Initially she organised her relationship to analysis along systematic lines. Her relationship with her analyst was to do with logic and empirical observation; ideas were abstract and perceptions objective; common sense prevailed. Her references to herself were all objective, and she expected objective explanatory interpretations. If the analyst made efforts to suggest that he had emotional importance for her as a physical being his suggestion was politely rebuffed; if he persisted he became a threat. He then became, she said, like her mother, and the patient believed that he was going to insist on telling her how she felt and claiming that he knew that she loved him really and that it was only her wickedness that made her deny it. The patient made it clear that if he were to acquire these characteristics of her mother she would have no choice but to leave. There was always a threat that she might try to leave life at the same time by committing suicide. In the early periods of analysis anything which drew attention to the analyst's physical presence or her physical presence disturbed her. From the time she began the analysis she had accompanied it with a variety of physical therapies in parallel: yoga, massage, osteopathy, special movement classes. The person administrating these had to be anonymous and relatively silent. When one enthusiastic physical therapist offered a psychological comment during treatment she promptly left. I was reminded of this when reading recently that in Indonesia, where teaching any religion other than Islam is illegal, the Government enforces silence in yoga classes because it is allowed only as a physical exercise and words which might possibly be resonant with Hinduism must not be spoken.

In my second clinical case the enemy was objectivity. The patient's first person subjective view of the analytic situation and the analyst's attempted third person objective view were believed to be mutually destructive. The only hope lay in the adoption of the patient's subjective view and the patient believed that any effort by the analyst to assert something different would crush her sense of self. I have spoken elsewhere of such situations and their relationship to the primitive Oedipus situation (Britton, 1989); I emphasised then that the only way out of such an impasse is by the analyst's recognition of the nature of the problem and his own internal struggle to accommodate both his own and the patient's psychic reality: that is the necessary work which needs to be done. Otherwise the analyst tries to compel the patient to do this and since it is the patient's inability to do this that has created the problem in the first place this is fruitless. It is a great deal easier for an analyst to describe this than to do it. It was a failure of mine to contain such a situation that first really acquainted me with the dimensions of this problem and the violence that it could unleash.

In this case it led to a re-enactment of the psychic catastrophe that had caused her intrapsychic problems in the first place. The re-enactment of a primitive psychic catastrophe followed a comment of mine which was meant to be a helpful interpretation but which my patient took to be a moral pronouncement. I said to her that she wished to have a physically contiguous and continuous relationship with me and was trying by various efforts to give herself the sense that this was so. I then added that this would not serve her well because it required my eternal presence and that what she needed was to take in some verbal understanding from me so that she had it available inside her.

She thought I had attacked her only mode of relating to me and sought to substitute for it my religion that I would now impose on her. As she saw it I was forbidding the one kind of link she believed in and demanding that instead she accept my words as gospel truth and the only source of good.

Her reaction to this was violent. She communicated powerfully her feeling of exclusion and her hostility to my ideas by breaking the window and smashing things in the room. This certainly left in both transference and countertransference a sense of resultant desolation. It left her without any link to an outside figure for her quintessential self and any attempts on my part at this juncture to establish verbal connections led to further severances. Her solution to this was to form a relationship to me that excluded those elements she could not tolerate and it is the character of this relationship that I am calling "idolatry". I was as an idol, the source of all good, but as a source of "the word" I was anathema.

As I thought further about these two clinical situations I found through experience of similar cases that in the first situation hyperobjectivity reigned, in the second hyper-subjectivity, and that what was feared as potentially catastrophic was the integration of subjectivity with objectivity. This meant in the first that identification with the third object's viewpoint resulted in elimination of subjectivity in favour of what was taken to be objective reality, and that in the second hyper-subjective mode nothing should contradict the patient's subjective beliefs. The important point I want to make is that both of these defensive organisations were meant to prevent the recognised coexistence of more than one psychic reality. What was required was perfect understanding, perfect symmetry. In the first case this was to be achieved by suppression of the subjective self in favour of the reality of the other, in the second elimination of the reality of the other's mind. In the first case ruthless self-suppression was adopted in order to conform to what was perceived to be the psychoanalytic counterpart to revelation, God's word. In the second the psychoanalytic counterpart to acts of terrorism was used to control or eliminate the analyst's mind.

The development of a third position, that is, one from which the subjective self can be observed, so that one can see oneself while being oneself, is a necessary preliminary to the sceptical position I have referred to. When belief is attached to a phantasy or idea, initially it is treated as a fact. Realising that it is a belief and not a fact depends on viewing the belief from outside the belief system. This depends on internal objectivity, which in turn depends on the individual finding a third position from which to view his or her subjective belief about the object concerned. In the model I am proposing subjective belief comes first, before objective evaluation or reality testing. *Objective evaluation* may use external perception, in reality testing, or it may simply involve correlation internally with known facts or related beliefs. The *internal objective evaluation* of a subjective belief is particularly crucial in situations where direct perceptual confirmation is not possible. It depends on two processes both of which provoke resistance. One is the correlation of subjective and objective points of view and the other is the relinquishment of an existing belief. The former involves the *Oedipal triangle* and the latter *mourning*.

A state in which belief is treated as knowledge is usually described as omniscience and the resultant beliefs as delusions. However, in my scheme of things, initially beliefs are taken to be facts and I would not describe this as delusional but naïve, just as I would not call infantile mentation psychotic just because adults who continue to use it are psychotic. It would be more useful to describe as delusion belief that is treated axiomatically as knowledge even though it runs counter to perceptible reality. By this criterion the papal court that tried Galileo was deluded: the physical evidence of the solar system was available, but we could say that the pre-Copernican geocentric believers were not deluded, just mistaken.

My starting point in this business of considering belief was, like Descartes, the realisation that without question I had held in the course of my life fallacious beliefs. Descartes wrote in *First Meditation*: "Some years ago I was struck by the large number of falsehoods that I had accepted as true in my childhood, and by the doubtful nature of the whole edifice that I had subsequently based on them" (Ayer & O'Grady, 1992, p. 111). We are born believers and our development consists as much in relinquishing old beliefs as acquiring new ones. The relinquishment of old ideas seems to cause more difficulty than the acquisition of new ideas.

We need to believe in order to act and react and a good deal of the time we have to do so without knowledge. I think that we believe in ideas in a similar way that we "cathect" objects. A belief is a phantasy invested with the qualities of a psychic object and believing is a form of object relating. I think belief as an act is, in the realm of knowledge, what attachment is in the realm of love. The language of belief is clearly cast in the language of a relationship. We embrace beliefs or surrender to them; we hold beliefs and we abandon them; sometimes we feel that we betray them. There are times when we are in the grip of a belief; held captive by it; feel persecuted by it, or are possessed by it. We relinquish our most deeply held beliefs, as we relinquish our deepest personal relationships, only through a process of mourning. It is my observation that those people who have difficulty relinquishing objects have difficulty relinquishing beliefs. So we are at the mercy of our beliefs.

But can we do without our belief function, by which I mean our innate, initial capacity to treat as fact that which is only an assumption? Clearly not: we rely on it to give us a sense of security outside the range of possible observation of our beloved or necessary objects. Our species can travel far and for long periods because of this capacity; when it falters we are anxious. When we encounter individuals who do not possess a belief function or have lost it we see what dreadful consequences follow from that. It is in essence the ability to relate to probability as we would to certainty, a capacity that varies in individuals.

David Hume, as I wrote earlier, outside his study could treat his *natural beliefs* as if they were facts despite his academic conviction that this could never be justified.

Hume's radical scepticism was what prompted Kant into embarking on his philosophical journey that led to the German metaphysics of the nineteenth century. France also was entranced by Hume's thinking but England largely ignored it, just as it ignored German ideas for more than half a century, contenting itself with Locke's empiricism, Bentham's utilitarianism, scientific progress, and religious sentiment. Exhausted by the Napoleonic wars and frightened by the French Revolution it turned its back on big ideas, until that is the beginnings of analytical philosophy which took science as the source of real knowledge and reason as its handmaid. Actual science by this time, particularly in physics, had gone ahead by ignoring philosophy altogether, with relativity and quantum mechanics transcending it not with machines but with mathematics, so producing an account of the world that we cannot actually imagine as it transcends our perceptually space-based imagery and our logical reasoning.

The analytic philosophers of the twentieth century felt the need to reconcile their rigorous logical reasoning with actual science despite Hume's propositions. Reading A. J. Ayer's painstaking account of this reminded me of yet another form of psychopathology, Asperger's syndrome. I do not mean for a moment to imply that Ayer, a very human everyday sort of man, was a sufferer but that the means he had to employ to give logical justification to the inductive reasoning that we all take for granted has just that quality. It is interesting that when using what Russell called the demonstrative method to guarantee the uniqueness of any event or object necessary to avoid a collapse into tautology, Ayer said, "It has the great disadvantage of making the whole system egocentric, in as much as every spatio-temporal reference is tied to the context of the speaker" (1973, p. 143). Again I think we can say that we have met this not in theory but in practice in our consulting rooms. Our narcissistic borderline patients would stand transfixed at the only place they believe to be safe, that is at their "point of view". As Ayer puts it, speaking of the logical impossibility of justifying our system, "[T]here is nothing exterior to it and we cannot stand in the void" (ibid.). Our Asperger's patient who lacks the subjective gestalt of what we rightly or wrongly take to be reality tries to construct in logic what we accept without thought. In doing so some such personalities arrive at more free and original systems of thought than most of us can manage, tied as we are to our commonsense view of things.

The void, or a chaos of contradictions, is what is feared by many who do not securely possess a subjective assumptive sense of reality based on a function that enables them to treat beliefs as facts and probabilities as certainties. They do not have that ontological security that enables individuals to remain confident of their own existence and to believe in some ultimate reality even though their knowledge of it is necessarily very partial.

Many people want a total model of the universe, a *Weltanschauung*, and religion provides one. Freud emphasised that the *Weltanschauung* of science differs from its religious and metaphysical predecessors which provided a construction that solved all the problems of existence with an overriding hypothesis that finds a place for everything. He acknowledged that science assumes the uniformity of the explanation of the universe but only as a programme, the fulfilment of which is relegated to the future. "It asserts", he wrote, "that there are no sources of knowledge of the universe other than the intellectual working over of carefully scrutinised observations—in other words what we call research—and alongside of it no knowledge derived from revelation, intuition or divination" (1933a, pp. 158–159). Psychoanalysis shares this world view with science and in this respect it differs from religion.

This view of knowledge is not a popular one, and so science only gets general acceptance by bribing the population with promises of advantageous applications. A scientific approach to mental life is even less popular and therefore we find ourselves as psychoanalysts trying to justify our existence in a similar way. If we can promise to remedy mental illness, increase productivity, or bring peace to the world we may hope to be tolerated. Religious belief on the other hand is popular; it is usually only displaced by secular counterparts that offer similar certainties in exchange for simple faith: secular certainties such as Marxism or fascism.

These certainties will not survive empirical observation and so empirical observation will be condemned, as Galileo was condemned. He was not condemned for accepting the Copernican system as an intellectual exercise but only for claiming to prove it. Where mathematics and astronomical observation contradicted divine revelation in the scripture then said the papal authorities the concept of the earth rotating round the sun must be an error. This abnegation of new knowledge by the authority of the papacy is familiar to everyone; less familiar perhaps is the same claim of "divine authority" on an individual basis. So called "Inner Light" religions such as the Anabaptists arose in the Reformation and later flourished in proletarian Britain in the early nineteenth century. William Blake, the poet and artist, embraced in an extreme way such a subjectivist belief system and testified to it in the most brilliant and eloquent ways. This is described in Chapter Twelve.

Blake's description of reason (Urizen) as an adamantine rock which his imaginative self (Los) smashed has great meaning for me because of clinical experiences with some patients. I can remember being treated as just such an adamantine rock and similar violence followed, smashing parts of my room. I learnt the hard way not to be such a rock of ostensible reason in such a context where the patients' belief system, their psychic reality, was equated with their psychic existence. Like Sartre they felt their subjective reality would be destroyed by another's objective view of them. Their ontological existence was identified with their epistemological system. This I think also applies to some religious groups and some religious states of mind, and I think this must be what is meant by fanaticism, when belief is regarded as a matter of life or death. One could say they cannot change their minds without fear of losing their minds.

Our natural beliefs, that is, those that like Hume's inform our daily lives, I have described in Chapter Four. They come first; they do not wait for logic or demonstration, and they are often accompanied by supernatural beliefs. Those who lack the usual capacity for assumptive, natural belief in the continuity of things, try to substitute magical thinking, superstitious practices, and some form of fetishism or idolatry. Others rely on the word of God for their guarantee of survival.

In the twentieth century analytic philosophy became the handmaid of science and metapsychology the servant of political philosophy. Science marched ahead and departed from logical philosophy and from common sense producing an account of the physical world that is abstract, mathematical, and unimaginable. It leaves a gap between the scientific account of the universe and the experience of life outside the laboratory. This will tempt even more people to fill that gap with religion. If it can be religion with a strong dose of scepticism that may be safe enough for it is scepticism that makes religion safe. But it requires triangular space so that subjective belief can be observed internally and be seen as belief and not fact.

Bertrand Russell, committed to science and logic, saw scepticism as the only defence against religion or "a welter of conflicting fanaticisms" (1946, p. 744). Among the holders of these he included Nietzsche who said God is dead and replaced him with super-man. Russell quoted from Shakespeare where King Lear claims to be such a man:

> I will do such things—
> What they are yet I know not—but they shall be
> The terror of the earth.

"This is Nietzsche's philosophy in a nutshell," Russell said (ibid.).

We today are afraid that there are others all too ready to share this philosophy; so exchanging God for super-man might not be such a good idea.

CHAPTER TEN

The severance of links

Bion's development of his concept of "attacks on linking" was part of his exploration of the "psychotic personality" and the part it played in psychotic and non-psychotic neurotic disorders (1957, 1959). He considered that a "psychotic personality" coexisted with a "non-psychotic personality" in psychotic disorders and in severe neuroses, with the psychotic personality dominant in the former and masked by a more dominant neurotic pathological organisation in the latter. He also suggested that in the psychotic personality projective identification substituted for regression in the neurotic personality. The projective identification he refers to in this passage is of an extreme order in which the ego's experience of reality is fragmented and projected, sometimes into inanimate objects. Thus the elements provided by Freud's reality principle, "that is to say, consciousness of sense impressions, attention, memory, judgment, thought" (Bion, 1959, p. 47) are lost through projection.

At the heart of this psychotic personality is "an omnipotent phantasy that is intended to destroy either, reality or the awareness of it, and thus to achieve a state that is neither life nor death" (p. 46). In other words, if the mental representation of something could be eliminated, this would eliminate the actual "something". In this supposed state of affairs, the eradication of awareness of an object by elimination of its psychic representation would mean the actual link, the sensory connection to an object, would be wiped out. An example from the history of psychoanalysis, namely the case of Anna O as described by Breuer, can illustrate it. She had negative hallucinations: that is, in one phase of her disorder she was completely perceptually unaware of the physical presence of anyone other than Breuer (Freud & Breuer, 1895d). This was part of a severe case of what was rightly described as hysteria; the use of a psychotic mechanism in this neurosis is complementary to Bion's theory and perhaps illustrates the usefulness of the "old fashioned" psychiatric term hysterical psychosis. Anna O omnipotently created a subjective, perceptual world that only included herself and her doctor.

In the cases Bion wished to characterise as manifesting features of the psychotic personality the connections with anything outside the "self" were completely eliminated. Within my own psychiatric experience the clinical picture most resembling this was in some cases of catatonic schizophrenia in the days before antipsychotic medication became commonplace. In this state, which could be regarded as resembling a theoretical state of primary narcissism, there is imputably only a central self with no relationships other than to itself. But if one posits, as Melanie Klein did, that an object relation exists from the outset of any self-awareness this self-self relationship was originally a self-object relationship. In "attacks on linking" the omnipotent phantasy has changed subject-object into subject-subject: fusion instead of connection. We could describe this in terms of projective identification.

If we take the first normal object relationship to be container/contained, that is self inside object or object inside self, once this has been replaced by self-self it is then a self contained by itself or a self containing itself. I believe we experience the mind as in the body or the body as in the mind, and that in normality there is an alternation of these alternative models. If there is an omnipotent phantasied disconnection, the mind is only inside itself, the body is nothing more than an idea of the mind. The outside world similarly is only an extension of the self; there is no outer world or indeed any other world.

I have never had the opportunity of analysing a schizophrenic patient in a catatonia, which one can think of as the ultimate disconnected state of mind. The psychotic patients one does meet clinically in analysis are more partial in this respect and one relies on contact with the non-psychotic personality of the patient, which as Bion said is always a latent or hidden presence in psychotic illnesses. In my own experience with a chronic psychotic patient, in an analysis that lasted twenty years, this was so. In her case her mind was dominated by thoughts that came from her psychotic personality and in effect they terrorised her non-psychotic self. Her neurotic solution was to produce a pathological organisation that aimed to rid herself of all her thoughts since she took all thought as arising from her psychotic personality. Her methods were to attempt to eradicate her thoughts by physical sym-bolic evacuations such as flushing the toilet repeatedly, closing doors behind herself innumerable times in the hope of leaving her mind in the room she had just left, and so on. This was a defensive use of projective identification that alas created an even more dangerous external world for her that was full of her evacuated thoughts. She managed to place this world outside the small portion of London she and I both inhabited, which meant she could live within it but not travel anywhere beyond it. She was undiagnosable according to psychiatrists who, taking her symptomatology to be obsessive-compulsive, tried to locate her as such but were unable to accommodate her multiple delusions within the diagnosis. Once in analysis the chronic psychosis was evident and the defensive rituals could be seen for what they were.

However, our lack of access to the ideas of the essential, psychotic personality, such as that described by Bion, can be compensated by considering the works of artists committed to a similar system as an ideology.

One such was William Blake in the early eighteenth century and another Kazimir Malevich in the twentieth century. The latter wrote of his new movement,

> Suprematism is the beginning of a new culture. Our world of art has become new, non-objective, and pure. Everything has dis-appeared; a mass of material is left from which a new form will be built ... The artist can be a creator only when the forms in his picture have nothing in common with nature. (1915, p. 1)

The iconic picture of this movement was his "Black Square" (1915) which eliminated all forms in the picture that the visiting eye expected to see.

Similarly Blake wrote, "I must invent a system or be enslaved to another man's." He regarded his imagination as the divine source, the creator, and he regarded *belief* as the act of creation; self-doubt he saw as destruction:

> If the Sun & Moon should Doubt
> They'd immediately Go out.
> (Keynes, 1959, p. 433)

He saw belief as truth; formed by imagination and not received by perception; not seeing is believing but believing is seeing. He wrote that, "... vision is the world of imagination: is Eternity. Vision is all that exists." And he claimed, "Mental things alone are real." The eye is an organ for projection not perception:

> This Life's dim Windows of the Soul
> Distorts the Heavens from Pole to Pole
> And leads you to Believe a Lie
> When you see with, not thro' the Eye
> (ibid., p. 753)

Belief, treated as fact, was for him the limiting membrane of an otherwise bottomless void, the only curb on the total mental disintegration that followed the act of creation. Creation, he thought, resulted in the catastrophic separating out of the intellect from within the primal unity of the self. The intellect he saw as attached to the illusion of a finite, measurable physical world. He had two versions of this catastrophe. In the first, Urizen (a pun on your reason), who is the personification of intellect, creates a fathomless void in the personality by detaching himself from the whole body of the eternal self by his attachment to the world of physical sensation. In the second account of catastrophic creation, Los, imagination personified, is confronted with an impenetrable, material, objective world created by Urizen, a solid non-fluctuant object. Los was driven wild with impatience by this black, adamantine, impenetrable, reality rock created by Urizen. So he smashed it to pieces thus producing a bottomless abyss into which he then fell.

So we have in the first version the subjective account of a prenatal quiescent psychic unity ruptured by the part of the mind that by linking itself through the senses to the physical world tears itself off, leaving a chasm within the self. In the second account the infant imagination in its frustration and antipathy to reality represented as an impenetrable, black, cold object of adamantine hardness smashes it to fragments and then falls into the abyss thus created.

> Falling, falling! Los fell & fell
> Sunk precipitant heavy down down
> Times on times, night on night, day on day
> Truth has bounds. Error none: falling, falling:
> Years on years, and ages on ages
> Still he fell thro' the void, still a void
> (ibid., p. 258)

This second version of Blake's strongly resembles that described by Melanie Klein as the destructive attack on the internal object resulting in states of mental fragmentation. "The mechanism of one part of the ego annihilating other parts ... I suggest underlies *world catastrophe*," she wrote (1946, p. 24). Bion in several of his writings emphasised this notion of Klein's that the patient attacks his object with such violence that not only is the object felt to disintegrate but also the mental apparatus of the person delivering the attack. This poetic account by Blake describes this and the ensuing symptomatology in an extraordinarily vivid way.

The mind then falls into the abyss of unknowingness thus created. As it falls it labours to produce a belief system that it can treat as the truth, the "bounds" it needs to arrest its fall. Earlier Blake had propounded a dictum of absolutist subjectivity so that "Everything possible to be believed is an image of truth" (1825–27, p. 8); so the belief system the mind creates "as an image of the truth" serves as its own safety net and remedy for chaos and the void. The enemies of this belief are therefore the enemies of self-existence and the creators of chaos. The sceptics, *the Questioners* as Blake calls them, are therefore the enemies of the mind. Professional questioners such as empirical or natural philosophers are the agents of Satan: Bacon, Locke, and Newton in particular—Bacon for seeking truth through reason as opposed to revelation; Locke for his emphasis on learning through experience as opposed to Blake's belief that "Man is a garden ready planted and sown" (Johnson & Grant, 1979, p. 443); and Newton for formulating the laws of nature in a material universe that Blake abhorred and proof by mathematics which he despised. "Science is the Tree of Death" wrote Blake (Keynes, 1959, p. 777). The only safety net and remedy for world catastrophe is psychotic delusion. We as analysts would do well to bear in mind the way Blake sees the realistic or reasoning doubters as the dangerous agents of chaos. Analysis with its inbuilt scepticism can be seen to be dangerous to patients with such beliefs and they will try to avoid analysis even whilst in it. They may well be attached to the analyst in a positive transference while treating analysis as potentially catastrophic.

Blake interestingly offers us two alternative reasons for disconnection from the internal representation of the psychical world and these one could see similarly as psychoanalytic alternatives. In one the primal unity, we might call it "primary narcissism", is ruptured by an attachment in the first object relationship. There is now a gap in the inner world. In other words an object relationship divides the self. In the second the primacy of the infinitely, immediately satisfying pleasure principle is challenged by the adamantine nature of reality with its finite space and measurable time. This arouses such fury that its internal connections are smashed. Frustration or rather intolerance of frustration is the provocation and destruction is its outcome. Is the individual's disconnection from the outside world and its internal representatives regression or destruction? Freud appeared to think of regression whilst Abraham saw it as intolerance of object love and implied aggression. This difference of opinion persists in psychoanalytic theorising, resurfacing in different views of narcissistic disorders as defensive and libidinal or destructive.

The difference I think disappears if instead of thinking of narcissism as primary and object love as secondary they could be seen as coincident and conflicting from the beginning. But I would propose that they are not both positive drives or impulses, that *it is not narcissism versus socialism* as Bion puts it in *Attention and Interpretation* (1970). Narcissism can be seen not as a force in its own right but as a negative reaction to connection to objects because they are not identical and thus arouse a psychic immune response of hostility. It could be said to be not auto-eroticism but autoimmunity. It applies physio-pathologically when part of the body is wrongly identified as alien and is attacked by the immune system. So it could be with mental parts of the self, which are attacked by the mental immune system. It is as if a body such as a nation or a religion decides that part of its population was alien and decides to annihilate it.

Anyway, in whatever way it arises, connection is the provocation and the psychotic solution is disconnection. This drastic solution results in psychotic illness in which survival is dependent on unacknowledged others or some sort of compromise that evades complete disconnection whilst avoiding the catastrophic object relationship. A "pathological organisation" (Steiner, 1987) producing a neurosis or personality disorder is one such compromise. I described one particular example where self and object are psychically interchangeable as if they were two halves of one object in Chapter Five. What is the relation of Bion's concept of the psychotic personality characterised by severance with the familiar psychoanalytic concept of narcissism as a force or predisposition in the personality that opposes object relations?

This notion of disconnection in psychosis, that is in dementia praecox (schizophrenia), was first put forward by Karl Abraham in 1907. He wrote to Freud, "I believe what in cases of chronic mental illness is called dementia is nothing but the patient shutting himself away from the world, the withdrawal of libido from persons and objects" (Abraham & E. Freud, 1965, pp. 6–7). He added, "The insufficient development of object-love appears to be an inhibition in the maturation of the personality.". Freud readily agreed with this as can be seen in their correspondence; their first letters were written before Abraham actually met Freud. Freud saw this withdrawal of libido as regression to auto-eroticism in individuals, "who had inadequately completed the necessary development from auto-erotism to object-love". Abraham's account, though it does not contradict Freud, sounds more like an active repudiation of object relations and in this respect it is more like the subsequent, much later, version Bion based on Melanie Klein's work and adopted in "Attacks on Linking" (1959). The wording of his title implies an aggressive motive, which is why I prefer the less committed term "severance" as it leaves open the aetiology and possible reasons for the disconnection.

If we adopt Klein's model of infancy in which introjection is the beginning of extra-uterine life then we can see disconnection as preventing it. Klein wrote of introjection as "… in his phantasy he takes into himself everything which he perceives in the outside world … Not only the mouth … for instance, the child breathes in, takes in through his eyes, his ears, through touch and so on" (1936, p. 291). By disconnection there is no introjection, it is cancelled by severance, or to be more precise if introjection is a phantasy a counter-phantasy eliminates it. Disconnection is a process, which in phantasy annihilates all phantasies based on introjection. This would then resemble what has been described as "primary narcissism" which in earlier psychoanalysis was thought of as a pre-object related developmental phase. I am suggesting in line with Klein and Bion that it is a narcissistic aspiration not a developmental stage, that total disconnection from the world of external perception and internal sensation is due to an effort to be rid of object relatedness. In the world of the arts I have talked of Blake's claim that imagination and not perception should create the world. And in the last century Malevich strove to free painting from nature and to substitute abstract forms. His black square was composed by the elimination of anything but black. "The artist can be a creator only when forms in his picture have nothing in common with nature." And his "white forms against a white background" represented "a final liberation from the world of visible forms". These paintings are the artistic counterpart to negative hallucinations as manifest by Anna O. Even hallucination might be rendered invisible such is the urge to eliminate perception of natural forms. A psychotic patient had what Bion calls "invisible hallucinations". "He sat up," said Bion, "and stared intently into space. I said he seemed to be seeing something. He reported that he could not see what he saw" (1962b, p. 95). I would like to suggest that "narcissism" in the sense of the abolition of object relations is not primary but is reactive; that it is a psychic immune response to the ingestion (introjection) of objects that are not identical with the self. In its most extreme form, which Bion characterises as the psychotic personality, it also annihilates those aspects and functions of the ego that connect to the object.

As Klein said, if one part of the ego annihilates another that produces what is phantasied to be the "world catastrophe". The non-psychotic personality therefore regards the psychotic personality as its greatest threat and the defensive organisations it produces in an attempt to safeguard itself are manifest as neuroses and neurotic characteristics. These include what are often described as narcissistic disorders and it is as well for analysts to keep in mind the defensive function of these pathological organisations which the patient regards as necessary to prevent domination by the psychotic personality. This means that some patients believe that their pathological organisation is keeping madness at bay, and analysis therefore is felt to be a potential threat and the analyst a mad enthusiast. One such patient of mine with a narcissistic disorder and a history of an adolescent psychotic breakdown dreamt, when underway in his analysis, of driving a car along a cliff and a traffic policeman confidently waving him onwards over the cliff edge.

It was not difficult to see that I was the policeman and the cliff edge was the analysis. In such circumstances the positive transference may attach the patient to the person of the analyst but not to the analysis. In such cases the patient's fear that free association and acknowledgement of transference love will lead to madness needs to be exposed repeatedly. Only after this has been worked through does a freer relationship develop between the patient and his/her hidden thoughts.

In this chapter I have emphasised the underlying or manifest psychotic urge to disconnect arising from psychic allergy to foreign objects and the perceptions they give rise to. This is not the only source of opposition to introjection that may manifest itself during analysis: there is an alternative which one could describe as traumatic. In this sense it is similar to the differentiation I made between destructive and libidinal narcissism following Herbert Rosenfeld (Britton, 2008). This traumatic object-phobia arises I believe where the fear is of intrusive projective identification by the object, probably with a history of such projection in the infantile primary relationship and subsequent analogous experiences in the Oedipal situation. This scenario needs to be distinguished from the attacks on links described by Bion, referred to in this chapter as severance.

It is not too difficult to do this in analysis but it is difficult to describe as it is largely a matter of countertransference affect. Roughly speaking I would say the first situation is found in narcissistic and psychotic disorders, while the latter is found in hysteria; each has its own characteristic countertransference. In this respect it returns us to the very first discussion of these differences by Abraham: "In the one case the libido is withdrawn from objects, in the other it cathects objects in an excessive degree. On the one hand there is a loss of the capacity of sublimation, and on the other increased capacity for it (Abraham, 1908). The theoretical understanding of these states has been enlarged and changed, and I am suggesting a further addition with the notion of *psychic atopia*, but the phenomenology remains the same. This I think is a testimony to clinical psychoanalysis and the discoveries it makes.

CHAPTER ELEVEN

What made Frankenstein's creature into a monster?

"The scientist does not study nature because it is useful to do so. He studies it because he takes pleasure in it and he takes pleasure in it because it is beautiful. If nature were not beautiful it would not be worth knowing"

—*Poincaré*, 1952, p. 22

No written work of the Romantic school of literature has been of greater interest to twentieth-century scholarship. Almost as much literary fascination has been aroused by its genesis as by the novel. This was at a house party in the holiday home of Lord Byron on Lake Geneva in June 1816: present at the Villa Diodati with Lord Byron were the poet Percy Bysshe Shelley and Mary Godwin, as she was then, plus her stepsister Claire Clairmont and Dr. Polidori, a young doctor. Mary Shelley's own account is in the preface she wrote fifteen years later for the 1831 third edition of her novel, *Frankenstein*. Through her journal and letters and the diary of Dr. Polidori we know a good deal more about that time in Geneva than she disclosed in the preface.

Much has been written on *Frankenstein* from various points of view and it is not my intention to summarise or supersede these but as an analyst to explore Mary Shelley's relationship to it. In order to do this I treat the preface of 1831 as if it was like a preliminary consultation, with the other parts of her history and the novel itself as what might have emerged in a subsequent analysis. So, starting at this imaginary consultation ...

We know that her husband, the poet Shelley, drowned in a boating accident in Italy nine years before in 1822, and that she has one surviving child, Percy, now aged twelve. Four years ago in 1826 she published another science fiction novel, *The Last Man*, in which a pandemic wiped out all humanity leaving one man anticipating his own death sitting in the ruins of Rome. She began writing *The Last Man* in 1824, the month Byron died in Greece, so then of the Geneva summer party only she and Claire were still alive. Dr. Polidori had poisoned himself with prussic acid aged only twenty-one.

So let us imagine that Mary Shelley is consulting us in 1831, when at thirty-four she is about to publish the third edition of *Frankenstein*. She comes with a question on her mind: "How did she an eighteen-year-old girl come to think of and dilate upon so very hideous an idea?" As I would with a consultation I will underline what seems significant in the preface and also what facts are missing, such as those that would have emerged in a subsequent analysis.

She begins by saying, that as the daughter of two persons of distinguished literary celebrity she thought she should be a writer. Her father William Godwin was the famous radical author of *An Enquiry Concerning Political Justice* (1793), and her mother Mary Wollstonecraft of the equally famed *A Vindication of the Rights of Woman* (1792). Her husband, Mary said, was very anxious that she should prove herself worthy of her parentage and enrol herself on the page of fame. Though as a child she wrote stories these were realistic and nothing as compared with her secret daydreams, which were at once, more fantastic and agreeable; they were her refuge when annoyed and her deepest pleasure when free. She emphasises that she was not confined to her own identity in these daydreams; she became others and so peopled them with creatures far more interesting than her own sensations.

In the summer of 1816 the group in the Villa Diodati read German ghost stories to frighten each other. She remembers two of them as if they were told yesterday. One is of a lover who clasps his bride to whom he had pledged his vows only to find himself in the arms of the ghost of the woman he had deserted. The other is of the sinful founder of his race who is fated to bestow death on his beloved sons, when he kisses them; they "from the hour of the kiss withered like flowers snapped upon the stalk". At Byron's suggestion they agreed to invent a frightening story each. She adds that she listened to a discussion between Byron and Shelley on the basis of life and the hints of reanimation that galvanism had caused by producing movement in corpses. "Perhaps the component parts of a creature might be manufactured, brought together and endued with vital warmth," she says (Butler, 1994, p. 195).

This interestingly also describes her method as a writer. She makes a strong statement about the creation of fiction: "Everything must have a beginning ... Invention ... does not consist in creating out of void, but out of chaos; the materials must in the first place be afforded: it [invention] can give form to dark, shapeless substances, but [it] cannot bring into being the substance itself." In our terms, she is saying, the unconscious has to provide the raw material for "invention" to shape a story. This is very similar to Freud's idea of secondary revision making a narrative from dream elements, which he compared as analogous to a daydream. If we see this secondary revision like a daydream as a sort of closure, putting the lid back on unconscious phantasy, sometimes I think we could see it working in reverse. And I suggest that Mary's daydream of scientific experiment opened a door to phantasies of a dreadful scene of childbirth.

When she went to bed that night in the Villa Diodati this is what she describes, "I saw with shut eyes but acute mental vision, the pale student of unhallowed arts kneeling beside the thing he has put together." She saw, "... the hideous phantasm of a man stretched out and then on the working of some powerful engine show signs of life" (Butler, 1994, p. 196). She emphasises she was "*possessed*" by her *unbidden and uncontrollable imagination* far beyond reverie. This clearly was no daydream. I would call it *a night terror*; a sleep induced visual hallucination that persists on waking. Then she saw the artist rush away from his odious handiwork, and she describes how he hoped that sleep might abolish his horror and the silence of the grave abolish the hideous animated corpse. But when he opens his eyes behold the horrid thing stands at his bedside opening his curtains and looking at him with yellow, watery but expectant eyes. She opened hers with terror at this point but could not rid herself of her phantom.She tried unsuccessfully to distract herself by trying to think of a ghost story until, swift as light and as cheering, *she had the idea that what terrified her will terrify others*, that she needed only to describe the spectre that had haunted her midnight pillow to be free of it. She began the next day telling her story. This process that leaves her feeling cheery we would call projective identification, and Mary Shelley was a past master of it: in her daydreaming, her storytelling, and in the construction of her novels.

What she leaves out of this imputed consultation is of more significance than what is included. First, more on her "distinguished parentage": she was the only child of William Godwin and Mary Wollstonecraft but she never knew her mother as she died from puerperal sepsis eleven days after giving birth. She knew her only from her writings and her childhood daydreams as she often sat by her mother's grave. It was on her mother's grave that Shelley seduced her when she was sixteen.

Mary had an older half–sister, Fanny, whose father was Gilbert Imlay, an American who Mary Wollstonecraft lived with in Paris during the French Revolution and the subsequent Terror. He abandoned her when back in London, leaving her desperately suicidal. William Godwin helped her to recover and despite their mutual scorn of convention they married and Mary was the product of their union.

After his wife's death Godwin was determined to produce a proper "family" and he believed he had achieved this by remarrying when Mary was four. However, Mary detested her stepmother who brought with her two stepsiblings, Charles and Claire. Godwin thought he had created a happy family; what Mary thought he created was a hell on earth.

The presence of Claire Clairmont, her stepsister, is one of the most notable omissions from her recollected account of the Diodati party. There were in fact five of them and it was Claire who had engineered their presence, having seduced Byron a short time before in London. Also with them in Geneva was William, Mary's six-month-old baby. His name is of considerable significance: it was her father's name and until she was born it was her name, constantly spoken of by the expectant parents as they planned their son's education. Mary gave this name to her son, her second child, and it is the name she gives in her novel to Victor Frankenstein's little brother who is the Monster's first victim. Mary's first child was a girl who was born prematurely and died nameless a few days after birth. In her journal of March 1815 she wrote: "Dream that my little baby came to life again ... I awake and find no baby ... I thought that if I could bestow animation upon lifeless matter, I might in process of time renew life where death had apparently devoted the body to corruption" (Moers, 2012, p. 324). Her son William was born a year later.

When Shelley and Mary had eloped in 1814, two years before the holiday at Villa Diodati, they took with them Claire Clairmont: they became a ménage à trois of sorts. They were supposedly all advocates of "free love". "Otaheite philosophers" Claire named them, referring to the stories of the promiscuity of the newly discovered islanders of Tahiti. When they signed the hotel register at Chamonix they provocatively described themselves as "atheists" in the hotel register. But by 1816 Mary's idea of bliss was to be *without* Claire: she wrote to Shelley, "Give me a garden & *absentia Clariae* and I will thank my love for many favours" (Seymour, 2011, p. 165). There were other unmentioned, uncomfortable facts: when they eloped in 1814 Shelley had abandoned his wife and child when Harriet was five months into a second pregnancy.

So we have as unmentioned background facts to her nightmare her mother's death in childbirth, Shelley's abandonment of Harriet and his children, her experience of having a dead baby girl, the birth of a son to whom she gave her own prenatal name, and her increasing hostility to Claire. Overdetermination seems to be an understatement.

But I think the immediate provocation of the night terror is another omission: the drama that occurred during Byron's reading of Coleridge's poem *Christabel*. This we know from Dr. Polidori's diary: "LB repeated some verses of Coleridge's Christabel, of the witch's breast: when silence ensued & Shelley shrieking and putting his hands to his head, ran out of the room with a candle. [I] Threw water in his face and after gave him some ether. He was looking at Mrs. S & suddenly thought of a woman he had heard of who had eyes instead of nipples, which taking of his mind horrified him" (Seymour, 2011, p. 157).

Christabel is a strange, supra-natural, quasi-medieval epic written by Coleridge as a successor to *The Ancient Mariner*. Christabel, personification of virginal beauty, leaves her father's castle at midnight and goes to the wood where she rescues Geraldine, whom she takes to be a maiden in distress, who subsequently bewitches and seduces her. This is the passage that provoked Shelley's hallucination:

> "Beneath the lamp the lady bowed,
> And slowly rolled her eyes around;
> Then drawing in her breath aloud,

> Like one that shuddered, she unbound
> The cincture from beneath her breast:
> Her silken robe and inner vest,
> Dropt to her feet, and full in view,
> Behold! her bosom and half her side—
> A sight to dream of, not to tell!
> O shield her! Shield sweet Christabel.

This poem and Shelley's hysterical reaction were among the assembly of disturbing experiences, unconscious phantasies, guilty secrets, and wishful daydreams that joined together to become a horrifying night dream of which the dreamer, Mary, no longer had control. Like the student of unhallowed arts she just wished that it would go away. "He hoped that he might sleep and that the silence of the grave would quench forever the transient existence of the hideous corpse which he had looked upon as the cradle of life."

Her night terror begins its daytime transformation when the dreamer becomes the author with a story that will terrify others. The creature's development continues as she makes it into a novel. *Christabel* played a further part when two months later Shelley read it aloud, this time without incident. The poem has two elements of particular relevance to Mary's novel: one is motherlessness and the other is gaze.

In the poem Christabel said of her mother, "She died the hour that I was born." Gaze is also central in both *Christabel* and the novel. Coleridge, taking his cue from Milton, describes a transformation in Geraldine's eyes,

> … the lady's eyes they shrunk in her head,
> Each shrunk up to a serpent's eye,
> And with somewhat of malice and more of dread,
> At Christabel she looked askance.

"Askance" is the word used in *Paradise Lost* when Satan looks on at Adam and Eve making love.

What do we think is passing through Mary's mind listening to Shelley read this together with Claire, as she hears Sir Leoline proposing to adopt Geraldine and when Christabel pleads to her father: "By my soul I do entreat/That thou this woman send away"?

From night terror to novel

Mary dealt with her night terror by turning it into a short story and then over nine months into a novel. In this Victor Frankenstein, ambitious young scientist, creates a living man from bits and pieces but when his creation actually comes to life he is horrified by its appearance and flees. He hopes to escape into sleep but he walks into a nightmare: there he meets and embraces his fiancée Elizabeth but at the first kiss she is transformed into the rotting corpse of his dead mother with grave worms crawling in her shroud. When, horrified, he wakes he sees the creature at his bedside looking at him expectantly with outstretched hand. In horror Frankenstein rushes off again. From then, like Coleridge's Ancient Mariner, he "doth walk in fear and dread/ and having once turn'd round walks on/and no more turns his head;/ because he knows a frightful fiend/doth close behind him tread".

From July 1816 Mary worked on the novel while concurrently reading *Paradise Lost* and finished it in May 1817. A great deal happened in those nine months. They returned to England to relative poverty and to two suicides. Mary's half-sister Fanny, who felt excluded from the Shelley entourage, killed herself, and Harriet Smith, Shelley's abandoned wife, drowned herself. Shelley and Mary married in December 1817, despite which Shelley failed in court to gain custody of his two children. On the positive side the Shelleys' marriage, though scorned as a bourgeois concession by Shelley and Claire, reconciled Mary with her delighted father from whom she had painfully been estranged since her elopement. The Leigh Hunts, Keats's main supporters, befriended them and in their cheerful, child-filled home dominated by Marianne Leigh Hunt, Mary experienced real happiness. She conceived again in December.

The novel

The novel has a complex form. There are three narrators: Victor Frankenstein the scientist; his creation the Monster; and Robert Walton who relays all their stories to his sister by letter. Walton does this while trying to find an unprecedented north-west passage through the Arctic ice. The unusual structure and ambience of the novel only resembles one other, *Wuthering Heights*, which was written thirty years later by another great daydreamer, Emily Brontë. Muriel Spark's apt biographical comment that until she wrote *Wuthering Heights* Emily Brontë did not know herself (Spark & Stanford, 1996 p. 13). I think apply even more to Mary Shelley and *Frankenstein.*

We know from Mary's account of her daydreaming method that she inhabits three characters of her novel: she speaks for them and they speak for her. I think Robert Walton, the intrepid Arctic adventurer, is an old daydream character from her childhood years in Scotland. Victor Frankenstein, the second narrator and the new Prometheus is modelled on Shelley, Byron, and William Lawrence, the controversial professor of evolutionary anatomy. The third and by far the most eloquent voice is that of the Monster, and he speaks for Mary's unconscious, saying things she does not really know about herself. He does so in two major passages: in the first, accusingly he addresses Victor Frankenstein who created him and rejected him; in the second, over the dead body of Frankenstein he explains his own destructiveness, his suffering, and his guilt.

His first speech, some years after his disastrous birth, follows his first two crimes, the murder of the boy William, Victor's little brother, and his culpable incrimination of the nursemaid Justine, wrongly judged and executed. The central provocation of both these crimes is a locket worn by William with a picture of his dead beautiful mother. "No mother had blessed me with smiles and caresses," said the Monster. "Remember," he said to Frankenstein, "I am thy creature; I ought to be thy Adam but I am rather the fallen angel ... I was benevolent and good, misery made me a fiend. Make me happy and I shall again be virtuous ... Will no entreaties cause you to turn a favourable eye upon thy creature ... you my creator abhor me; what hope can I gather from your fellow creatures ... they spurn and hate me." He argues that the hateful, horrified eye turned on him as the newborn creature makes him a fiend.

The Monster explains that after leaving his birthplace in Frankenstein's rooms he eventually had found a family living in a cottage on which he could spy unseen. There with a mixture of observation and idealisation he had learnt language, history, and human relationships. He then found some books, *Paradise Lost, Plutarch's Lives, and the Sorrows of Werther* (the key precursors of the Romantic writers), that formed the basis of his self-education. It was the horrified rejection of him by this ideal family when he finally plucked up courage to approach them that inflamed his anger. "From that moment", he said,

"I declared everlasting war against the species. If I cannot inspire love I will cause fear." The Monster's proposed solution is for Frankenstein to create a bride for him who would reciprocate his love and thus render him benign. "If any being felt emotions of benevolence towards me, I should return them a hundred fold ... I would make peace with the whole kind ... my creator make me happy; let me feel gratitude towards you for one benefit."

Frankenstein is reluctantly persuaded by this promise and prepares himself to do this, in remote Scotland. At the last moment when he is about to give life to this newly created female while watched through the window by the Creature he changes his mind and furiously destroys his work. The Monster, enraged, cries out, "Shall each man find a wife for his bosom, and each beast have his mate, and I be alone? Remember," he says, "I shall be with you on your wedding night."

There are then two more murders: Clerval, Victor's ideal, bosom friend, and Elizabeth, his bride, on their wedding night before their marriage was consummated. This radically changes the story: up to this point Frankenstein was haunted by the Creature; now as his pursuer he became the hunter and the Monster the hunted. We do not meet the Monster again until Robert Walton finds him crouched over the dead body of Frankenstein who died on board his ship.

Victor's last effort had been to inspire Robert and his crew by his rhetoric to persist in their hazardous mission to their near certain death. Despite the rhetoric Robert Walton turned for home and survival rather than heroic, fatal, failure.

The Monster, speaking over the dead body of Victor, who had died of exhaustion in vain pursuit of him, says, "In his murder my crimes are consummated ... O Frankenstein generous and self-devoted being what does it avail that I now ask thee to pardon me." The Monster describes how he was driven to a terrible revenge when Frankenstein, who destroyed his hopes of marital fulfilment, planned to marry himself. "When I discovered the author of my existence dared hope for happiness ... then impotent envy and bitter indignation filled me with an insatiable thirst for vengeance." "Evil thenceforth became my good," he says, quoting Satan in *Paradise Lost*. But he claims that though he inflicted pain on Frankenstein, "He suffered ... not the ten thousandth portion of the anguish that was mine during ... its execution. A frightful selfishness hurried me on, while my heart was poisoned with remorse. My heart was fashioned to be susceptible of love and sympathy; and when wrenched by misery to vice and hatred, it did not endure the violence of the change without torture ... I was the slave not the master of an impulse, which I detested, yet could not disobey."

And yet there is a flourish of final masochistic triumph as the Monster leaves the ship planning to die by fire. "Farewell Frankenstein ... Blasted as thou wert, my agony was still superior to thine; for the bitter sting of remorse will not cease to rankle in my wounds until death shall close them for ever."

Discussion

It gives a sense of the literary context in which she wrote Frankenstein to bear in mind it is contemporaneous with Jane Austen's *Pride and Prejudice*. It has been said that this *Frankenstein* turned the genre of fashionable superstitious gothic novels into science fiction. It was the first novel to be written by a woman contemporaneously with her experience of childbirth. Mary actually was very fond of children but imaginatively describes the absolute horror of perinatal rejection for both mother and child.

The antithesis of Wordsworth's infant babe who "nursed in his mother's arms ... doth gather passion from his mother's eyes", is the Creature who looks expectantly only to see horror and hatred in them. This she unhesitatingly suggests means that he will only repeat this experience. There is then an interlude in the account of her Creature's mental development that follows Locke's ideas and her father's "Benthamite" views. These psychologically optimistic ideas are rudely interrupted by the next major experience of rejection by the Creature that leads to his war on the species.

As we listen to her Monster speaking of his experience we hear the philosophical voice of David Hume rather than John Locke: "Reason is the slave of the passions." Natural beliefs inform daily life not golden reason, says Hume. "I was the slave not the master of an impulse, which I detested yet could not disobey," says the Monster. In his first speech we could say he was in the paranoid schizoid position, in the second he was in the depressive position. In the novel his account reminds us that Melanie Klein's first description of the depressive position was of a psychotic version. "But [it is] the ego's hatred of the id which is paramount in this phase ... it is the ego's unconscious knowledge that the hate … may … get the upper hand … which brings about the sorrow, feelings of guilt and the despair which underlie grief" (1935, p. 270).

In Mary Shelley's novel only Robert Walton of her three narrators survives: Victor Frankenstein dies after urging everyone on the ship to continue their suicidal mission; the Monster leaves the ship to embrace a self-inflicted painful death. Only Robert Walton the intrepid explorer remains, judiciously but reluctantly turning for home. The Monster of the deep unconscious is returned to ashes, Frankenstein the ego ideal is safely housed in idealised posterity, and Robert, the ego, steers back into more mundane and safer waters.

Mary Shelley's is not a "gothic novel". Unlike them it is not a supernatural horror story: the creator's horror is the beginning of a natural tragedy, one when a mother looks at a newborn baby and sees a monster. This Monster is not super-human, he is all too human. Her daydreaming has not provided an escape from her unconscious, it has opened the door to it. However, she finds a new home for horror in the minds of her readers. "And now," she says on launching a new edition, "once again I bid my hideous progeny go forth and prosper. I have an affection for it, for it was the offspring of happy days, when death and grief were but words, which found no echo in my heart." Though worse followed, including the death of two more children and of her husband, can we really accept her claim of happy days when death and grief were just words? Is not this retrospective denial? As her extraordinarily wise Monster says, "Of what a strange nature is knowledge! It clings to the mind, when once it has seized on it, like lichen on the rock. I wished sometimes to shake off all thought and feeling; but I learned that there was but one means to overcome the sensation of pain and that was death."

CHAPTER TWELVE

The preacher, the poet, and the psychoanalyst

The preacher, the poet, and the psychoanalyst are all concerned with the mental or spiritual reality, which is with psychic reality, which I regard as the individual's conscious and unconscious beliefs. However, the preacher, the poet, and the psychoanalyst can be distinguished from one another by their different approaches to belief. The preacher expounds what he considers it necessary to believe, the poet seeks to discover and communicate his own beliefs, and the psychoanalyst aims to discover and explore the beliefs of his patients. In practice the analyst might be tempted to become the preacher, trying to convert his patient, or to be the poet, exploring his own psychic reality by attributing it to his patient. But when doing either of these things he has forfeited his role of analyst.

Milton and Blake, the two poets with whom I am concerned in this chapter, were both given to preaching. I am going to suggest that they both urged one belief system when they were preaching and revealed another when functioning poetically. The religious belief systems that they preached were different, but both were the counterpart to what in modern psychoanalytic terms we call defensive organisations, built on counter-belief systems. That is, belief systems erected to counter an already existing underlying belief of a catastrophic kind. I suggest that Milton, as a preacher, produced a theological counterpart to Rosenfeld's description of destructive narcissism, but as a poet he revealed his fear of a theological nightmare that resembles the inner world of the melancholic. Blake as preacher puts forward a belief system that resembles Winnicott's description of the true/false self organisation (1960) and as a preacher he advocates a return to primary, libidinal narcissism as salvation. However, as a poet he conveys a fear of the void, with the world fragmented and the self annihilated such as we meet in the analyses of borderline personalities. What I am suggesting is that the pathological organisations (Steiner, 1987) of these narcissistic disorders are defences against catastrophic states of mind and analogically that Milton and Blake's counter-belief systems as preachers are defences against the psychic reality they reveal as poets.

I am making three assumptions. One is that poetry at its best provides a special route to psychic reality; another, that thanks to psychoanalysis we can treat theological statements as metapsychological descriptions, and a third that religious belief is not restricted to formal religions, but is a type of believing. I am also suggesting that a good poem is a better guide to psychic truth than a good sermon: but only to poetic truth. What do we mean by that?

"Poetry gains body from beliefs," Louis MacNeice wrote, [but] "... not necessarily because they are the right beliefs. It is not the absolute, or objective, validity of a belief that vindicates the poetry; it is a gross over-simplification to maintain that a right belief makes a poem good and a wrong belief makes a poem bad" (1941, p. 6).

My own answer to the question, how can a misguided belief be the basis of a great poem?, would be to make a distinction between a true representation and the representation of the truth. Both Milton's and Blake's poetic accounts are true, vivid, and insightful descriptions of various mental states even though the beliefs informing these states may be misguided.

With this in mind I want to look at Milton's *Paradise Lost* as a study of his mental state and at Blake's extraordinary determination to change Milton's mind posthumously by writing an alternative poetic account in which Milton figures as a character. It is as if Blake wanted to cure Milton of being Milton.

Milton was not only a great poet, he was a considerable essayist and pamphleteer particularly in matters of religious doctrine. Yet he turned to poetry to attempt what was of most importance to him, to "justify the ways of God to men" (Scott Elledge, 1975, p. 9). Given the circumstances of his own life at the time of writing *Paradise Lost*, Milton's belief that God ordained all things and also that he was a personal, loving, merciful God gave him a lot to explain.

Milton was blind from the age of forty-four, he had lost two wives in childbirth, and his only son died as a one year old; Cromwell, his political leader, was dead, his beloved republican administration defeated, and the monarchy restored; some of his friends were executed and he only just escaped the same fate. His three adolescent daughters resented him and were a grave trouble to him and he to them. In the words he gave to the blind Samson, of his *Samson Agonistes* (1671), we can see his state of mind:

> Now blind, disheartened, shamed, dishonord, quelled,
> To what can I be useful? Wherein serve
> My nation, and the work from heaven imposed!
> But to sit idle on the household hearth,
> A burdenous drone, to visitants a gaze,
> Or pitied object?
> (Campbell, G., 1990, p. 525)

In this state he wrote *Paradise Lost*. He began with an invocation of the poetic muse and a prayer to the Creative Spirit whom he equates with the very God, whose ways he aims to justify. His poem, he says, "pursues/Things unattempted yet in prose or rhyme" (Scott Elledge, 1975, p. 8).

As the poet, Milton appeals to his God for inspiration, so that as an advocate he might defend him as his client. This makes us, his readers, the jury. It also goes to the heart of the problem as a plea from Milton to God to give him the means so that he can defend him (William Empson quoted from *De doctrina* that Milton had written).

> There are some who, in their zeal to oppose this doctrine [predestination], do not hesitate even to assert that God himself is the cause and origin of evil. Such men, if they are not to be looked upon as misguided rather than mischievous, should be ranked among the most abandoned of all blasphemers. An attempt to refute them would be nothing more than an argument to prove that God was not the evil spirit. (Elledge, pp. 613–614)

So he scorns to do this in prose but in *Paradise Lost* he turns to poetry to accomplish this, trusting that it will give him direct access to the divine parent whom he so desperately wants to defend from these accusations

> … what in me is dark
> Illumine, what is low raise and support;
> That, to the highth of this great argument,
> I may assert Eternal Providence,
> And justify the ways of God to men.
> (ibid., p. 9)

Milton wished to fortify his belief that his God loved him and that God's omnipotence was unqualified and unimpaired. To do this he needed to account for his suffering at the hands of God and for the presence of evil in God's world. In his *De Doctrina Christiana*, written in Latin as two pamphlets, he functions as a preacher promulgating his beliefs and he seems quite satisfied by his explanations. Having dismissed atheism as self-evidently foolish he is left with the alternative belief that "… either God or some supreme evil power of unknown name presides over the affairs of men. But it is intolerable and incredible that evil should be stronger than good and should prove the true supreme power. Therefore God exists" (Elledge, 1975, p. 402). As to what God is like he simply states, "It is safest for us to form an image of God in our minds which corresponds to his representation and description of himself in the sacred writings, he could never say anything about himself which was lower or meaner than his real nature" (ibid., pp. 402–403).

Milton firmly declared that his beliefs about God's actions were entirely based on the Bible and on the Bible alone. This meant he had to justify God's curses on the men and women he had created such as those found in the book of Ezekiel:

> In the place where you were created, in the land of your origin, I will judge you. And I will pour out my indignation upon you; I will blow upon you with the fire of my wrath; and I will deliver you into the hands of brutal men, skilful to destroy. You shall be fuel for the fire; your blood shall be in the midst of the land; you shall be no more remembered; for I the Lord have spoken. (Holy Bible, Ezekiel 21 v. 28)

In psychoanalysis this is a familiar internal god; it is the superego of those unfortunate enough to suffer from melancholia. As Freud first described it:

> If we turn to melancholia (first), we find that the excessively strong super-ego rages against the ego with merciless violence, as if it had taken possession of the whole of the sadism available in the person concerned. Following our view of sadism, we should say that the destructive component had entrenched itself in the super-ego and turned against the ego. What is now holding sway in the super-ego is, as it were, a pure culture of the death instinct. (1923b, p. 53)

Freud also said, "To the ego, living means the same as being loved, being loved by the super-ego" (ibid., p. 58). Translated into theological language this reads as "Not to be loved by God is the same as death."

Some years ago I wrote a paper on the analyses of patients who had a seriously disturbed parent. I described in that paper the evolution of an unassimilated internal object opposed and hostile to these patients' normal ego functions. I called it an "alien object". If this internal enemy took position as the superego it acquired moral force and supernatural power. This often resulted in terrible indictments of worthlessness and death threats in the form of hypochondriacal convictions of fatal illness. This would be the equivalent of the theological nightmare that Milton attempted to dismiss. "But it is intolerable and incredible that evil should be stronger than good and should prove the true supreme power" (Elledge, 1975, p. 402). If this internal object could be dethroned, though it remains a disturbing presence, it loses its moral power. It is preferable to believe in the Devil than to think of oneself as created by a cruel and hostile God. From the latter there is no escape and indeed one cannot even want to escape, for there is nowhere to go to be saved. Such is, I think, the psychological force of the superego.

Freud commented, "The Devil would be the best way out as an excuse for God" (1930a, p. 120). Faced with the need to firmly establish belief in a just and loving God, Milton turned from prose to poetry. In order to exonerate God he changed the plot and made Satan a more central character than God. What changes the theological and psychological picture in *Paradise Lost* is the central presence in the poem of Satan. Psychoanalytically it changes the internal world described from that of melancholia to that which was described by Herbert Rosenfeld as "destructive narcissism" (Rosenfeld, 1971). The initial innocence of the subject self and the restoration of the superego, or internal god, as the source of goodness, is accomplished by the creation of another character; a destructive, evil interloper who seduces the ego from its natural propensity to worship and obey the superego. Our ancestral parents were supposedly prompted and seduced by Satan, who personifies envy and pride, and worships only himself. In psychoanalytic terms belief in the goodness of the internal parent/god of the superego is restored by the proposition that a destructive, narcissistic aspect of the personality exists that leads the naïve self into betraying his/her relationship to the source of nothing but goodness.

To take first the clinical formulation of Rosenfeld of destructive narcissism:

> In some narcissistic patients the destructive narcissistic parts of the self are linked to a psychotic structure or organisation which is split off from the rest of the personality ... the whole structure is committed to narcissistic self-sufficiency and is strictly directed against any object relatedness ... When narcissistic patients of this type begin to make some progress and to form some dependent relationship to the analysis, severe negative therapeutic reactions occur as the narcissistic psychotic part of the self exerts its power and superiority over the analyst, standing for reality, by trying to lure the dependent self into a psychotic omnipotent dream state which results in the patient losing his sense of reality and his capacity for thinking. (1987, p. 112)

In Milton's *Paradise Lost* we find Satan, personifying destructive narcissism, excluded from God's heaven, and determined to see his exile as a triumphant entry into his own diabolical narcissistic kingdom:

> ... Farewell happy fields ...
> Infernal World ...
> Receive thy new possessor—one who brings
> A mind not to be changed by place or time.
> The mind is its own place, and in itself
> Can make a Heaven of Hell, a Hell of Heaven ...
> Here we may reign secure, and, in my choice,
> To reign is worth ambition, though in Hell:
> Better to reign in Hell than serve in Heaven ...
> (Elledge, 1975, p. 16)

Starting with his own version of Christian theology and his own reading of the Bible, Milton elaborated an imaginative account of the fall in *Paradise Lost*. This has had such an impact that it is misguidedly taken by many people to be the one in the book of Genesis. He accounts for the suffering and death of mankind as punishment for our ancestors' sin of disobedience and for the existence of evil in the world by the presence of Satan, the fallen angel whose pride and envy led to defiance of God. He suggests that God's loving character is made manifest by his readiness to offer his divine son as a human sacrifice to be mocked, vilified, tortured, and unjustly executed. If we were to remove Satan from Milton's poetic account we would be left with humanity banished, unloved, and undergoing indefinite punishment by God on grounds of ancestral disobedience. The tyrannical, cruel, and vengeful nature of Milton's God in *Paradise Lost* has been commented on by a number of authors, notably William Empson (ibid., pp. 605–618). As I suggested, this baleful picture of the occupant of the seat of divine judgement is not unfamiliar if we translate it into our own psychoanalytic terms. Substituting the term superego for God we would have a perfect picture of the internal world of the melancholic.

However, as a poet in giving us this account Milton cannot resist giving us the history, adventures, and soul-searching of Satan. As a poet he inadvertently leads us to understand and identify with Satan as human whilst as a preacher he is seeking to demonstrate to us that he is evil personified. In *Paradise Lost* Satan is not an abstract power but someone who suffers intense envy and jealousy and is trapped in eternal reprobation by his pride. In Book IV of *Paradise Lost* Milton surprisingly presents us with Satan as someone capable of feeling conflict and guilt. He had been destined to be the personification of pride and envy, and wholly evil; in psychoanalytic terms a part object, an object in which part is whole; a character manifesting only one quality. Instead Satan becomes a whole person experiencing conflict, remorse, and dread: not an object but a subject. And Milton in this passage anticipates what Melanie Klein was to call the depressive position.

In Book IV *of Paradise Lost*, after his journey from Hell Satan arrives on a mountain top from where, looking south, he can see Eden. His purpose is to revenge himself on God by tempting the primal couple to betray their creator. Milton reminds the reader of Satan's future identity as the dragon of the Apocalypse who will do battle with God for the soul of mankind. At the moment of his arrival on Niphates, fuelled by his rage, he is hell-bent on revenge and insulated by his indignation from doubt, dread, or pity: he is not simply in a rage he is outraged. His hurt pride reassures him that his pre-existing belief in the supremacy of his position need not be questioned, by telling him that he is wronged, usurped, and unnaturally deprived. While he continues to believe this he is protected not only from reproach but also from envy. However, at the moment of giving birth to his vengeful project something happens to him; that which,

> ... boils in his tumultuous breast,
> And like a devilish engine back recoils
> Upon himself ...

Satan recoils upon himself; in psychoanalytic language he ceases to project and finds that hell is within himself and is not his unjustly imposed prison. Suddenly,

> ... horror and doubt distract
> His troubled thoughts, and from the bottom stir
> The hell within him; for within him hell
> He brings, and round about him, nor from hell
> One step, no more than from himself, can fly
> By change of place: Now conscience wakes despair,
> That slumber'd; wakes the bitter memory
> Of what he was, what is, and what must be
> Worse; of worse deeds worse sufferings must ensue.
> ... I fell ...
> Warring in heav'n against heav'n's matchless King.
> Ah wherefore! he deserved no such return
> From me .... (ibid., pp. 85–86)

Milton also, like his character Satan, has "back recoiled" upon himself in the sense that he has looked inwards into his own human nature to find an explanation for Satan's continuing destructiveness. He does so in the vicissitudes and complexities of a depressive position compounded by despair and unbearable envy, and the "debt immense of endless gratitude". He makes Satan human, and in this short passage makes clear why this particular human cannot remain in the depressive position and is left with a choice between melancholia or the role of the destructive narcissist.

> Me miserable! Which way should I fly
> Infinite wrath, and infinite despair?
> Which way I fly is Hell; myself am Hell;
> And in the lowest deep a lower deep
> Still threat'ning to devour me opens wide,
> To which the Hell I suffer seems a heaven.
> O then at last relent: is there no place
> Left for repentance, none for pardon left?
> None left but by submission; and that word
> Disdain forbids me, and my dread of shame
> ... But say I could repent and could obtain
> By act of grace my former state; how soon
> Would height recall high thoughts, how soon unsay
> What feign'd submission swore! ease would recant
> Vows made in pain, as violent and void.
> For never can true reconcilement grow,
> Where wounds of deadly hate have pierc'd so deep;
> Which would but lead me to a worse relapse
> And heavier fall ...

Satan cannot bear the thought that if he repents and is forgiven he will once again be provoked by envy into a rebellious attack, and once again have to repent. He cannot imagine that he will be able to contain his feelings and integrate them with his acknowledged admiration and gratitude. So he re-dedicates himself to the active pursuit of destruction which promises triumph over the goodness which he believes he cannot sustain:

> So farewell hope, and with hope farewell fear,
> Farewell remorse; all good to me is lost;
> Evil be thou my good ... . (ibid., p. 88)

Even now Satan seems to need further and final provocation before committing himself to the destruction of mankind's future happiness. Milton provides it by having Satan witness the primal scene, that is, Adam and Eve making love:

> ... Aside the Devil turned
> For envy; yet with jealous leer malign

> Eyed them askance, and to himself thus plained.
> Sight hateful, sight tormenting! thus these two,
> Imparadised in one another's arms,
> The happier Eden, shall enjoy their fill
> Of bliss on bliss; while I to Hell am thrust,
> Where neither joy nor love, but fierce desire,
> Among our other torments not the least,
> Still unfulfilled with pain of longing pines.

This finally confirms him in his conviction that he is better off as the self-appointed ruler of destruction in hell than suffering the pangs of envy in the beauteous world.

In a few lines Satan restores his pride by scornfully imagining the unsuspecting couple's downfall and once his pride is re-established he is free from the torments of envious and jealous feeling:

> … Live while ye may,
> Yet happy pair; enjoy, till I return,
> Short pleasures, for long woes are to succeed!
> So saying, his proud step he scornful turned …. (ibid., pp. 99–100)

Pride is the fuel of his destructive narcissism and protects him from the infinite despair of his melancholia.

So I suggest Milton as a preacher seeks to justify the ways of God to men by interposing Satan, as the evil angel, between them. He offers us destructive narcissism, evil personified, as a defence against the despair of melancholia. However, as a poet he presents us with something different: an analysis of Satan as a tragic man. In the prose of his Christian doctrine Milton promulgates a somewhat fierce Protestant faith; in *Paradise Lost* he shows himself to be a great humanist poet of English verse.

Blake

William Blake was probably the first to suggest that Milton, his literary hero, was not really on the side of God but of Satan when writing *Paradise Lost*. Blake based this claim on the quality of the verse: he regarded the passages concerning Satan as sublime and those concerning the angels and heaven as mundane. He wrote: "Note. The reason Milton wrote in fetters when he wrote of Angels & God, and at liberty when of

Devils and Hell, is because he was a true Poet and of the Devil's party without knowing it" (1825–27, p. 6).

More than a century after Milton wrote *Paradise Lost* Blake set about trying to reverse it in his illustrated book *The Marriage of Heaven and Hell*. This can be most clearly seen by looking at the engraving later entitled *The Good and Evil Angels*. At first sight it appears that a good angel, white and fair, is protectively clasping an infant (representing mankind) to keep it from a bad angel, of dark coloration, who is pictured rising from the flames, where he is chained, to reach for the child. This would appear to illustrate the essence of Milton's account of the fall in *Paradise Lost* with Satan trying to get his clutches on infant Adam who is in the protective arms of a good angel. Blake's own explanation of his picture, however, is exactly the reverse. He says the ostensibly "good" white angel is a representation of diabolical, organised religion stealing infant mankind from the sources of energy within himself represented by the dark angel (ibid., p. 4).

According to Milton, Man's loss of Paradise was due to disobedience, but according to Blake it was a consequence of obedience. For Milton the fall results from the defiance of the reality and morality created by a just God. But for Blake, Man's fallen state is a consequence of his acceptance of the spurious reality of his senses and his compliance with the tyrannical morality of a false god.

Not satisfied with his correction of Milton's allegiances in *Paradise Lost* he makes him the central character in his own epic, the prophetic verses entitled *Milton Book the First* and *Milton Book the Second*. He subtitled it, in case we did not get the point, to "To justify the ways of God to Men". Blake addresses us in this poem at the outset as the narrator, whom he called "the Bard", an ancient British version of an Old Testament prophet who says:

> I am Inspired! I know it is Truth! For I Sing
> According to the inspiration of the Poetic Genius.
> (Keynes, 1959, p. 495)

The phrase "Poetic Genius" comes from Blake's tract *All Religions are One* in which he wrote "… all religions & as all similars, have one source. The true Man is the source, he being the Poetic genius" (ibid., p. 98). In other words Blake as a preacher tells us that the only source of truth is poetic genius. If we take my suggestion that poetic revelation is psychic reality we can paraphrase Blake as saying that psychic reality is *the only reality*.

The first book of *Milton* is preceded by a preface in which Blake makes clear that he is going to rescue mythic truth from misguided allegiance to Greek and Roman literature. As he puts it: "... the stolen and perverted writings of Homer & Ovid, of Plato & Cicero which all men ought to contemn." Even his literary heroes Shakespeare and Milton were infected by the general malady.

The two books are meant to replace Greek mythology with Blake's own. The hero is Milton, who is Ulysses, Prometheus, Hercules, and Jason all in one. Blake's other mythic characters include such as Albion, Los, Urizen, Orc, Enitharmon, etc. who are familiar from his other prophetic books. It parallels *Paradise Lost* with Blake's own version of the fall and Satan's journey through hell to earth. This time, however, Satan is an aspect of Milton, namely his false selfhood, which relies on biblical authority, reason, and memory and not on inspiration. Satan is Milton's false obedient self who bows to institutional religion. "I," says Milton, "in my Selfhood am that Satan: I am that Evil One!/He is my Spectre" (ibid.).

Blake's saga tells us of Milton casting off his spectral (false) self, and then meeting it again in the form of Urizen. Urizen is Milton's own reasoning power, whom he defeats in a wrestling contest on his way to earth. Milton then comes to earth in London by entering Blake's left foot. Blake, now full of Milton, accepts death pending resurrection and sees the coming of the Apocalypse.

Blake said more than once, "I must create a system or be enslaved by another Man's/I will not reason & compare: my business is to create." In his prophetic verses and *The Everlasting Gospel* he sets out to do that. Most of this prophetic verse is written in the preaching mode but it contains passages where the poet can be heard speaking through the preacher, revealing the state of mind that is prompting the urgent polemic. The character Milton's big speech is one such passage. He begins saying:

> There is a Negation, & there is a Contrary:
> The Negation must be destroyed to redeem the Contraries.
> The Negation is the Spectre, the Reasoning Power in Man,
> This is a False body, an incrustation over my Immortal
> Spirit, a Selfhood which must be put off & annihilated always.
> (ibid., p. 533)

Blake distinguishes between beliefs that are Contraries, and Negation. Contraries in Blake's Beulah (as in Freud's system Ucs.) can coexist without contradiction, whereas Negation refutes a belief by demonstration of its invalidity, in other words by reality testing. In *The Marriage of Heaven and Hell* Blake states that "Anything that can be believed is true." Contraries, therefore, are welcome, but the enemy is Negation.

> The Negation is the Spectre, the reasoning Power in Man.
> I come in Self-annihilation & the grandeur of Inspiration!
> To cast off rational Demonstration by Faith in the Saviour,
> To cast off the rotten rags of Memory by Inspiration,
> To cast off Bacon, Locke, & Newton from Albion's covering,
> To take off his filthy garments, & clothe him with Imagination!
> To cast aside from Poetry all that is not Inspiration.
> To cast off the idiot Questioner who is always questioning,
> who publishes doubt & calls it knowledge; whose Science is despair,
> Whose pretence to knowledge is Envy: whose whole Science is
> To destroy the wisdom of ages to gratify ravenous Envy. (ibid.)

In this passage he reveals his fearful belief that objectivity will destroy subjectivity, that the reality testing of belief, which he calls negation, will annihilate the true self. The psychic reality of the individual can be destroyed by any other reality opposed to it. The snag with this system is that there is not only material reality to contend with, there is another reality external to the self, namely that of the psychic reality of other people. These fears resemble those found in some patients in analysis, often referred to as "borderline", whom I would also describe as "thin-skinned narcissistic patients" (Rosenfeld, 1987, p. 274). In such patients the attempted integration of subjective being and objective thinking is believed to cause a psychic catastrophe. As it is an aim of psychoanalysis to integrate subjective experience and objective understanding, the very process of analysis is felt to be a threat to this group of patients. Until analysis has produced some modification, objectivity is believed to be the death of subjectivity. In the analysis this amounts to the psychic reality of the analyst being regarded as incompatible with the psychic reality of the patient: unless it is the same the mind of the other will be the death to the self. Blake had a solution to this: it was called Beulah, a place that corresponds to what John Steiner called "psychic retreats" (1993).

There is a place where Contrarieties are equally True;
This place is called Beulah. It is a pleasant lovely Shadow
Where no dispute can come.
Beulah is evermore Created around Eternity, appearing To
the inhabitants of Eden around them on all sides.
But Beulah to its inhabitants appears within each district
As the beloved infant in his mother's bosom round incircled
With arms of love & pity & sweet compassion.
(Keynes, 1959, p. 518)

In 1895 Freud drew attention to a state of mind which he described as the "blindness of the seeing eye" in which "one knows and does not know a thing at the same time" (Freud & Breuer 1895, p. 117). Later he was to use the noun *Verleugnung* to describe this phenomenon which Strachey translated as "disavowal" in three papers (1924e, 1927c, 1940e). In the last of these he wrote of it as a "half measure" in which "the disavowal is always supplemented by an acknowledgement; two contrary and independent attitudes arise and result in … a splitting of the ego" (1940e, p. 204). I suggested in *Belief and Imagination* (Britton, 1998) that there is a syndrome in which disavowal is not partial but all pervasive: what Helene Deutsch had called the "as if" personality (1942). In this pathological organisation disavowal is placed at the centre of the individual's mental life and characterises his whole relationship to the world. When it operates there is no outcome and therefore no consequences. No firm belief is established that cannot immediately be reversed. *Either and* rather than *either or* is the mode and inconsequentiality is the result. One could characterise the whole organisation as sustaining inconsequence by suspending belief. As in Blake, Negation does not exist and Contraries coexist. As he wrote in *The Everlasting Gospel*:

The Vision of Christ that thou dost see
Is my Vision's Greatest Enemy
Thine has a great hook nose like thine
Mine has a snub nose like to mine.
Both read the Bible day & night,
But thou readst black where I read white.
(Keynes, 1959, p. 748)

For Blake, Beulah was a realm of mild moony lustre, and soft sexual delusions and "a place where Contraries are equally True". It relieved mankind of those two important distinctions that condemn us to live in a fallen world: the differences of *gender* and of *generation*. Judging from his unpublished explicit erotic drawings and his textual references to *male-females* and *female-males*, hermaphroditism prevailed in Beulah. The fallen world of material reality he called "Generation", he also called it "Experience".

Blake unashamedly propounds as the route to salvation what in psychoanalysis has been called infantile megalomania. In this state, he claims, we are what we imagine we are and our imagination is our share of the divine. In our infantile innocence he argues we unself-consciously believe this and when redeemed will do so again. This state of mind he celebrated in his *Songs of Innocence*. The other part of that collection, *Songs of Experience*, is an altogether different matter. In these he brilliantly captures the cruelty of human nature and the horrors of Regency London.

> In every cry of every Man,
> In every Infant's cry of fear,
> In every voice, in every ban,
> The mind-forg'd manacles I hear.
> How the Chimney sweeper's cry
> Every black'ning Church appals;
> And the hapless Soldier's sigh
> Runs in blood down Palace walls.
> (ibid., p. 216)

In Blake's view experience does not teach, it corrupts, with its deprivation, pain, and provocation and compels innocent egocentricity into giving a place to envy, jealousy, and covetousness.

> What is the price of experience? do men buy it for a song
> Or wisdom for a dance in the street? No, it is bought with the
> price Of all that a man hath; his wife, his children.
> Wisdom is sold in the desolate market where none come to buy,
> And in the withered field where the farmer plows for bread in
> vain.
> (ibid., p. 290)

And yet Blake the poet will out even when Blake the preacher is about his business. The *Songs of Innocence* have charmed generations of poetry readers but for me they only come into their own in juxtaposition with the *Songs of Experience*.

> First *Songs of Innocence*: "The Divine Image" ...
> For Mercy has a human heart
> Pity, a human face:
> And Love, the human form divine,
> And Peace, the human
> dress.
> (ibid., p. 117)

> Now *Songs of Experience*: "A Divine Image" ...
> Cruelty has a Human Heart
> And Jealousy a Human Face;
> Terror, the Human Form Divine
> And Secrecy, the Human Dress.
> (ibid., p. 221)

For me the two taken together induce a sense of sadness and reflection rather than the bliss or catastrophe described in the prophetic verses. The mood is one that we often characterise as that of the normal depressive position as opposed to the despair of the melancholic depressive position described in *Paradise Lost*. For Blake, however, judging from his verse, there was an obstacle to his finding a place to his liking in the world of generation, where love is complicated by its separate sexes and generations, its envy, jealousy, and painful losses.

There is a hint of it in a poem he never published:

> What to others a trifle appears
> Fills me full of smiles and tears

And in a letter to a friend:

> O why was born with a different face?
> Why was I not born like the rest of my race?
> When I look each one starts when I speak, I offend;
> Then I'm silent & passive & lose every Friend.
> Then my verse I dishonour, My pictures despise, My
> person degrade & my temper chastise;

And the pen is my terror, the pencil my shame;
All my Talents I bury, and dead is my Fame.
I am either too low or too highly prizd;
When Elate I am Envy'd, When Meek I'm despise'd.
(Johnson & Grant, 1979, p. 461)

Summary

Blake, looking at Milton's justification of God to men in *Paradise Lost*, decides this will not do and on poetic grounds decides this is a defensive organisation. I concur with this on psychoanalytic grounds and identify the pathological, defensive organisation with that described by Herbert Rosenfeld as destructive narcissism. But when Blake reverses this he reproduces another recognisable defensive organisation, that of the true/false self model described by Winnicott. As preachers both Milton and Blake have given us verse form precursors of what in twentieth-century psychoanalysis were described as pathological organisations. Milton produces Satan to exonerate God, a bad self alongside an ideal self to protect him from believing in a cruel superego. Blake abolishes God the father, the superego, and substitutes the divine self, the idealised ego.

As poets they give us the possibility of seeing something of the states of mind that these systems were organised to keep at bay. In Milton's case it was a defence against melancholia, in his terms the fear of living in a world created and ruled over by a cruel, hostile god, in my terms the fear of an ego-destructive superego. In Blake's case it was a defence against the fear of psychic annihilation and falling forever in what he called the void outside existence, a place commonly referred to these days as a psychic black hole.

However, both as poets also present us with alternative possibilities which as preachers they appear to have rejected. Milton gives us Satan, capable of feeling guilt and remorse, briefly contemplating swallowing his pride. Blake gives us a world in his *Songs of Experience* that is a sadder and grimmer place than in the *Songs of Innocence*, less blissful than Beulah, but with the great advantage of being as real as it sounds.

CONCLUSION

To sum up I want to return to the beginning by saying that I think we develop models of the world in our minds and as psychoanalytic theorists we develop models of the mind. And I would repeat Bertrand Russell's comment, "In every writer on philosophy there is a concealed metaphysic, usually unconscious; even if his subject is metaphysics, he is almost certain to have an uncritically believed system which underlies his specific arguments." In other words a hidden model, and I would apply this to metapsychologists.

You may ask, whatever happened to the notion of unconscious phantasy in my description? The answer is nothing. Melanie Klein's model of a mind rich in unconscious phantasies remains in mine as the storehouse. What I have added is Bion's stages that are preliminary to phantasy, from the somatic and the perceptual apparatus to mentation, namely from beta to alpha elements. These alpha elements are the bricks from which phantasies are made. They become models in other words and I have added another stage in their evolution, the belief function that turns them into what are taken to be facts. In terms of Freud's 1915 model this takes place en route to the preconscious from the system Ucs. In his structural theory of 1923 the preconscious becomes the unconscious ego. Should these beliefs become conscious they could be

127

reality tested: it is the task of analysis to make then conscious. For the imputed facts to be seen as beliefs and not facts requires a third position in the mind from which subjective experience can be judged. This, as I see it, is an ego function to do with reality and truth and not one to be abandoned to the superego, which deals in moral values and/or wishful thinking.

Learning from experience that we need to change our ideas is resisted by our allegiance to our models, particularly if shared by our fellow members of whatever tribe: ethnic, religious, or intellectual. Beliefs may be overcome by reason and reality but if they are not relinquished they linger in the shadows waiting for a stray beam of light to resurface as one of Freud's *unheimlich* moments or as a superstitious event.

Since Newton's work mathematics has meant that a model of the world can exist independently of observation and experiment, thus of the psychobiological model-making which otherwise we impose on our observations. The further development of mathematical models through Einstein's theories of relativity and even more of those of quantum physics has enlarged the gap between these mathematical models and our "natural" bio-psychological models of the world. There is still a similar gap between subatomic physics and cosmology and to some extent between subatomic physics and molecular chemistry in living organisms.

I think we find the mathematically based models of quantum counter-intuitive because they are free of our psycho-biologically based models and indeed do run counter to them. In contrast to quantum models, cosmological speculation resonates in ways familiar to a psychoanalyst. When we imagine rockets entering the inner orbital space of other planets, or of feet treading on mother moon's surface, or of black holes being the places where new universes might be generated, we are on psychoanalytic home ground symbolically. Indeed, and as in our own field the conflicting models of black holes as creators or destroyers lend themselves to our conflicting views of the womb, it is the creator of new universes or the in-sucking gravitational monster denuding us of our planetary identity.

My notion is that when quantum biology produces new models of the brain there will be a similar gap between neuroscience mathematical models and psychoanalytic models of the mind.

Our task is to become more aware of the unconscious models that inhabit our patients' minds and at the same time to make ourselves more aware of the models that shape our theorising. There is an important change taking place in biology that has a bearing on our field. It is twofold: one is the emphasis on continuous change that takes place over time in DNA; another is on the modification of inheritability as a response to circumstance. Due to the indivisibility of life what applies to bacteria applies to us. As bacteria breed at incredible rates it is possible to see successive generations in very short periods of time and thus to see generational changes in days that take centuries in human beings. It looks as though bacterial genetic (DNA) coding is influenced by encounters with antibiotics rather than simply as was thought that antibiotic resistance was just a consequence of natural selection of random mutations. It has introduced the idea of natural genetic engineering, which is "the ability of living cells to manipulate and restructure the DNA molecules that make up their genome" (Shapiro, 2011, p. 2). If that proves to be the case it means that cells can change their genetic identity in reaction to the environment. It would seem likely to apply potentially to all body cells including neurons and their networks.

How encouraging it would be to think that learning from experience could apply to the brain and not just the mind.

REFERENCES

Abraham, H., & Freud, E. (Eds.) (1965). *A Psycho-Analytic Dialogue: The Letters of Sigmund Freud and Karl Abraham (1907–1926)*. London: Hogarth and the Institute of Psycho-Analysis.

Abraham, K. (1908). The psycho-sexual differences between hysteria and dementia praecox. In: D. Bryan & A. Strachey (Eds.), *The Selected Papers of Karl Abraham*. London: Hogarth, 1973.

Ayer, A. J. (1973). *The Central Questions of Philosophy*. London: Penguin, 1976.

Ayer, A. J., & O'Grady, J. (1992). *A Dictionary of Philosophical Quotations*. London: Blackwell.

Bion, W. R. (1957). Differentiation of the psychotic from the non-psychotic personalities. In: *Second Thoughts* (pp. 43–64). New York: Jason Aronson, 1967.

Bion, W. R. (1959). Attacks on linking. In: *Second Thoughts* (pp. 93–109). New York: Jason Aronson, 1967.

Bion, W. R. (1962a). A theory of thinking. In: *Second Thoughts* (pp. 110–119). New York: Jason Aronson, 1967.

Bion, W. R. (1962b). Attacks on linking. In: *Second Thoughts* (pp. 110–119). New York: Jason Aronson, 1967.

Bion, W. R. (1962c). *Learning from Experience*. London: Karnac, 1984.

Bion, W. R. (1965). *Transformations*. London: Karnac.

Bion, W. R. (1970). *Attention and Interpretation*. London: Tavistock.

Blake, W. (1825–27). *The Marriage of Heaven and Hell.* M. Plowman (Ed.). [Reproduced facsimile.] London: J. M. Dent & Sons, 1927.

Braithwaite, R. B. (1953). *Scientific Explanation.* Cambridge: Cambridge University Press.

Britton, R. (1989). The missing link: Parental sexuality in the Oedipus complex. In: J. Steiner (Ed.), *The Oedipus Complex Today* (pp. 83–101). London: Karnac.

Britton, R. (1993). Fundamentalismus und Idolbildung. In: J. Gutwinski-Jeggle & J. M. R. Rotmann (Eds.), *Die klugen Sinne pflegende.* Tubingen, Germany: Edition Diskord.

Britton, R. (1998). *Belief and Imagination.* London: Routledge.

Britton, R. (2003). *Sex, Death and the Superego.* London: Karnac.

Britton, R. (2008). What part does narcissism play in narcissistic disorders? In: J. Steiner (Ed.), *Rosenfeld in Retrospect.* London: Routledge.

Butler, M. (Ed.) (1994). *Frankenstein, or, The Modern Prometheus, the 1818 text.* Oxford: World's Classics, Oxford University Press.

Campbell, G. (1990). *John Milton Complete English Poems,* London, J. M. Dent.

Cohn, N. (1993). *Cosmos, Chaos and the World to Come.* New Haven, CT: Yale University Press.

Darwin, C. (1859). *The Origin of Species.* Oxford: Oxford University Press, 1996.

Darwin, C. (1871). *The Descent of Man and Selection in Relation to Sex.* London: Penguin, 2004.

Deutsch, H. (1942). Some forms of emotional disturbance and their relationship to schizophrenia. *Psychoanalytic Quarterly,* 11: 301–321.

Edelman, G. (2006). *Second Nature Brain Science and Human Knowledge.* New Haven, CT: Yale University Press.

Elledge, S. (1975). *John Milton: Paradise Lost (Second Edition).* New York: W. W. Norton.

Evans, I. H. (1970). *Brewer's Dictionary of Phrase and Fable.* London: Cassell.

Farmelo, G. (2009). *The Strangest Man.* London: Faber & Faber.

Freud, S. (1891). Psycho-physical parallelism. Appendix B to "The Unconscious" (1915e), *S. E.,* 14: pp. 206–208. London, Hogarth.

Freud, S., & Breuer, J. (1895d). *Studies on Hysteria. S. E.,* 2. London: Hogarth.

Freud, S. (1897). Extracts from the Fliess papers. Draft N, Letter 64, 31 May. *S. E., 1:* 255–257. London: Hogarth.

Freud, S. (1900a). *The Interpretation of Dreams. S. E.,* 4–5. London: Hogarth.

Freud, S. (1915b). Thoughts for the times on war and death. *S. E., 14.* London: Hogarth.

Freud, S. (1915e). The unconscious. *S. E., 14.* London: Hogarth.

Freud, S. (1919h). The "uncanny". *S. E., 17.* London: Hogarth.

Freud, S. (1920g). *Beyond the Pleasure Principle. S. E., 18.* London: Hogarth.

Freud, S. (1921c). *Group Psychology and the Analysis of the Ego. S. E., 18*. London: Hogarth.

Freud, S. (1923b). *The Ego and the Id. S. E., 19*. London: Hogarth.

Freud, S. (1924e). The loss of reality in neurosis and psychosis. *S. E., 19*. London: Hogarth.

Freud, S. (1927c). *The Future of an Illusion. S. E., 21*. London: Hogarth.

Freud, S. (1927e). Fetishism. *S. E., 21*. London: Hogarth.

Freud, S. (1930a). *Civilization and Its Discontents. S. E., 21*. London: Hogarth.

Freud, S. (1933a). New Introductory Lectures on Psycho-Analysis: Lecture XXXV, *S. E., 22*: 158–182. London: Hogarth.

Freud, S. (1940e). Splitting of the ego in the process of defence. *S. E., 23*. London: Hogarth.

Freud, S. (1950a). *Project for a Scientific Psychology. S. E., 1*. London: Hogarth.

Graves, R. (1992). *The Greek Myths*. London: Penguin.

Heisenberg, W. (1962). *Physics and Philosophy*. London: Penguin, 1989.

Holldobler, B., & Wilson, E. O. (2009). *The Superorganism*. Cambridge, MA: Harvard University Press.

Holy Bible (1952). Revised Standard Version. London: Collins.

Isaacs, A., Daintith, A., & Martin, E. (1996). *Concise Science Dictionary*. Oxford: Oxford University Press.

Johnson, M. L., & Grant, J. E. (1979). *Blake's Poetry and Designs*. New York: W. W. Norton.

Jones, E. (1953). *Sigmund Freud: Life and Work (vol. 1)*. London: Hogarth.

Keynes, G. (1959). *Blake Complete Writings*. Oxford: Oxford University Press.

Klein, M. (1928). Early stages of the Oedipus conflict. In: *The Writings of Melanie Klein, Volume I* (pp. 186–198). London: Hogarth, 1975.

Klein, M. (1935). A contribution to the psychogenesis of manic-depressive states. In: *The Writings of Melanie Klein, Volume I* (pp. 262–289). London: Hogarth, 1975.

Klein, M. (1936). Weaning. In: *The Writings of Melanie Klein, Volume I* (pp. 290–344). London: Hogarth, 1975.

Klein, M. (1946). Notes on some schizoid mechanisms. In: *The Writings of Melanie Klein, Volume III* (pp. 1–24. London: Hogarth, 1975.

Kuhn, T. S. (1962). *The Structure of Scientific Revolutions, 2nd edition*. Chicago: University of Chicago Press.

Lakoff, G., & Johnson, M. (2003). *Metaphors We Live By*. Chicago: University of Chicago Press.

Leavis, F. R. (Ed.) (1950). *Mill on Bentham and Coleridge*. Cambridge: Cambridge University Press.

MacNeice, F. L. (1941). *The Poetry of W. B. Yeats*. Oxford: Oxford University Press.

Maddox, B. (2006). *Freud's Wizard*. London: John Murray.

Malevich, K. (1915). Kasimir Malevich, "Suprematism". The Artchive, Google.

Mason, M. (Ed.) (1988). *William Blake*. Oxford: Oxford University Press.

Massicotte, W. J. (1995). The surprising philosophical complexity of psychoanalysis (belatedly acknowledged). *Psychoanalysis & Contemporary Thought, 18*(1).

McFarland, T. (1985). *Originality and Imagination*. Baltimore, MD: Johns Hopkins University Press.

Mill, J. S. (1859). *On Liberty*. G. Himmelfarb (Ed.). London: Penguin, 1974.

Moers, E. (2012). Female gothic: The monster's mother. In: J. P. Hunter (Ed.), *Frankenstein: Mary Shelley (2nd edition)*. New York: W. W. Norton.

Pears, D. (1971). *Wittgenstein*. Glasgow: Fontana Modern Masters.

Pinker, S. (2007). *The Stuff of Thought*. London: Allen Lane.

Poincaré, H. (1952). *Science and Method*. New York: Dover.

Rey, H. (1979). Schizoid phenomena in the borderline. In: E. B. Spillius (Ed.), *Melanie Klein Today, Volume I*. London: Routledge, 1988.

Rosenfeld, H. (1971). A clinical approach to the psychoanalytic theory of the life and death instincts: An investigation into the aggressive aspects of narcissism. In: E. B. Spillius (Ed.), *Melanie Klein Today, Volume I* (pp. 239–255). London: Routledge, 1988.

Rosenfeld, H. R. (1987). *Impasse and Interpretation*. London: Routledge.

Russell, B. (1928). *Sceptical Essays*. London: Routledge, 1996.

Russell, B. (1946). *History of Western Philosophy*. London: Routledge, 2005.

Ryle, G. (1949). *The Concept of Mind*. London: Penguin.

Selincourt, E. de, & Darbishire, H. (Eds.) (1940). *Wordsworth Poetical Works*. Oxford: Oxford University Press, 1969.

Seymour, M. (2011). *Mary Shelley*. London: Faber & Faber.

Shapiro, J. A. (2011). *Evolution: A View from the 21st Century*. Upper Saddle River, NJ: FT Press Science.

Smolin, L. (2013). *Time Reborn*. London: Allen Lane.

Sophocles. *The Theban Plays*. E. F. Watling (Trans.). London: Penguin, 1947.

Spark M., & Stanford, D. (1996). *Emily Bronte her life and work*, London, Peter Owen.

Steiner, J. (1987). The interplay between pathological organisations and the paranoid-schizoid and depressive positions. *International Journal of Psychoanalysis, 68*: 69–80.

Steiner, J. (1993). *Psychic Retreats*. London: Routledge.

Thesiger, W. (1987). *The Life of my Choice*. London: Harper Collins.

Trotter, W. (1916). *Instincts of the Herd in Peace and War*. London: Scientific Book Club.

Untermeyer, L. (Ed.) (1961). Alexander Pope, An Essay on Man, II. In: *The Golden Treasury of Poetry*. London: Collins.

Winnicott, D. W. (1960). Ego distortion in terms of true and false self. In: *The Maturational Processes and the Facilitating Environment* (pp. 140–152). London: Hogarth, 1965.

Wordsworth, W. (1807). *Intimations of Immortality*. S. Gill (Ed.). Oxford: Oxford University Press, 1984.

Wordsworth, W. (1850). *The Prelude, 1799, 1805 & 1850*. J. Wordsworth, M. H. Abrams, & S. Gill (Eds.). New York: W. W. Norton, 1979.

INDEX